BE MORE COWBOY

Wrangling Wisdom from the Wild West

ABBIE HEADON

HarperCollins*Publishers*

HarperCollins*Publishers*
1 London Bridge Street
London SE1 9GF

www.harpercollins.co.uk

HarperCollins*Publishers*
Macken House, 39/40 Mayor Street Upper
Dublin 1, D01 C9W8, Ireland

First published by HarperCollins*Publishers* 2025

1 3 5 7 9 10 8 6 4 2

© HarperCollins*Publishers* 2025
Illustrations © David Andrassy
Cowboy icons by rawpixel.com on Freepik
Design by seagulls.net
Extract from Gene Autry's Cowboy Code © Autry Qualified Interest Trust
and The Autry Foundation. Reprinted with permission.

Abbie Headon asserts the moral right to be identified as the author of this work

A catalogue record of this book is available from the British Library

ISBN 978-0-00-879972-4

Printed and bound in the UK using 100% renewable electricity at CPI Group (UK) Ltd

All rights reserved. No part of this publication may be reproduced, stored in a retrieval system, or transmitted, in any form or by any means, electronic, mechanical, photocopying, recording or otherwise, without the prior written permission of the publishers.

Without limiting the exclusive rights of any author, contributor or the publisher of this publication, any unauthorised use of this publication to train generative artificial intelligence (AI) technologies is expressly prohibited. HarperCollins also exercise their rights under Article 4(3) of the Digital Single Market Directive 2019/790 and expressly reserve this publication from the text and data mining exception.

This book is produced from FSC™ certified paper and other controlled sources to ensure responsible forest management.

For more information visit: www.harpercollins.co.uk/green

Contents

INTRODUCTION: HOWDY, STRANGER! 4

1: A LONG TIME AGO IN THE WEST 7

2: THE COWBOY CODE 27

3: LEGENDS & LORE 45

4: WORDS FROM THE RANGE 61

5: RANCH LESSONS 77

6: STOIC IN THE SADDLE 95

7: HOME ON THE RANGE 111

8: THE STAGE, THE PAGE, & THE SILVER SCREEN 127

9: A COWBOY CHORUS 145

10: WHEN THE WORK'S ALL DONE 161

SO LONG, PARTNER: A COWBOY FAREWELL 175

THE COWBOY is one of the most easily recognized figures in the world, thanks to the classic outfit of boots, jeans, and a wide-brimmed hat, but there's so much more to cowboy life than simply style. What is it that draws us back to the way of the cowboy time and time again, in films, books, television shows, and fashion?

The answer, like all good answers, is both simple and complex. Simple, because we know that cowboys stand for the values of bravery, resilience, independence, and camaraderie, all in the context of some of the most stunning landscapes on the planet. Complex, because the idea of the Wild West was founded through conflict with the Indigenous people of North America, and its legacy impacts Native Americans to this day.

Perhaps we are drawn to cowboys because in an increasingly online world the pull of wide-open landscapes and adventures on horseback, with no algorithms or AI chatbots in sight, is ever more appealing. Instead of virtual-reality experiences, we long for real dirt on our boots and a crackling campfire to sit around in the evening, instead of a glowing screen.

Whatever draws you to the cowboy way of life, *Be More Cowboy* is here to take you on a cattle drive through the history, wisdom, icons, and humor of the knights of the Wild West. So, let's saddle up and head out onto the trail. *YEE-HAW!*

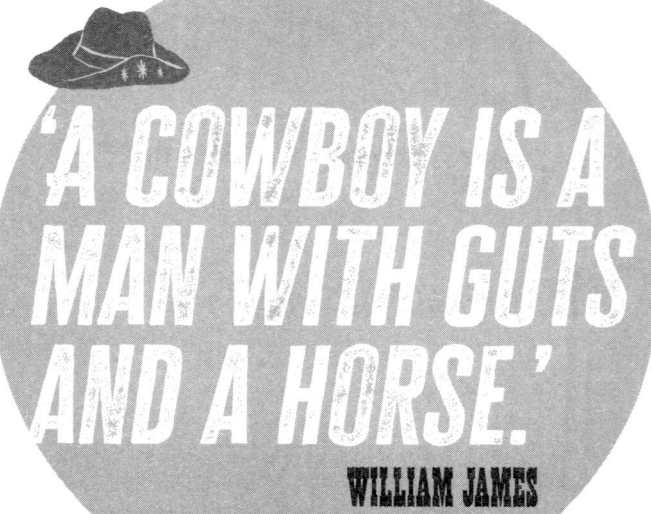

A Long Time Ago in the West

WHEN DID THE WILD WEST BEGIN?

It's hard to pinpoint an exact birthdate for the Wild West, but there are some key events that created the conditions for its beginnings. At the start of the nineteenth century, US army officers Meriwether Lewis and William Clark were sent by President Thomas Jefferson to explore the Louisiana Purchase, a vast parcel of land that had been acquired from France in 1803. The Lewis and Clark Expedition took place between May 1804 and September 1806, covering approximately 8,000 miles from Missouri, out to the Pacific Ocean, and back again. Then, in 1848, the United States signed the Treaty of Guadalupe Hidalgo with Mexico, in the process gaining 55 per cent of Mexico's territory. This land became the present-day US states of

California, Nevada, and Utah, as well as most of Arizona, Colorado, and New Mexico, plus a portion of Wyoming. The result of this huge expansion of the United States was that there was now an unimaginably large territory for Americans to explore and exploit. This land, lying mostly to the west of the 98th meridian, became known as the Wild West.

A SHORT HISTORY OF COWBOYS

The origin of the cowboy stretches back to the Spanish settlers who brought long-horned cattle to Mexico from Spain. The men who herded and drove the cattle were called *vaqueros*, a Spanish word derived from *vaca*, or 'cow.' These original cowboys came from diverse backgrounds, including Native American, African American, and *mestizo* (Native American and Spanish ancestry).

With the expansion of the cattle industry northwards and the transfer in the mid-nineteenth century of Mexican lands to the United States, more and more Americans, many of Scots–Irish ancestry, joined the cattle trade, learning the roping techniques that their Mexican forebears had developed.

Contrary to the images we often see in classic movies, as many as 25 per cent of all cowboys were Black. More recent films and television shows have increased the

representation of cowboys of color, but their contribution to cowboy history is often still underestimated.

What about cowgirls? Women played a key role in settling the West, taking on a lot of the hard work of running ranches and driving cattle, even though their contributions are sometimes overlooked in the more male-dominated interpretations of cowboy life on our pages and screens. When Wild West shows became popular in the late nineteenth century, women starred as sharpshooters and rodeo riders. Turns out there's nothing a cowboy can do that a cowgirl can't!

In this book, 'cowboy' refers to cowboys of all genders, because as history shows, there are no barriers to being a true cowboy.

WHAT IN THE BUCKAROO?

There's a wide range of words that mean 'cowboy.' The Spanish word *vaquero* was soon anglicized to become 'buckaroo,' a term widely used in the Great Basin and California. Other names for 'cowboy' include 'cow poke,' 'cow punch,' and 'cow puncher.' These names all describe the job of prodding cattle with long poles to make them move into, or out of, loading chutes or freight cars.

ACTIVITY

GIVE YOURSELF A COWBOY NAME

If you weren't blessed with a name that sounds like it should be out roaming the open prairie under a starry sky, don't worry! This cowboy name generator will give you all the dust-caked swagger you need to carry your head high at any ranch or rodeo.

Use the chart below to find the first name that goes with your date of birth and the last name that matches the month you were born in, and you'll be dandy. All the names are gender-neutral, so cowgirls, cowboys, and cowtheys can all get in on the action.

It's great to meet you, friend! I'm Riley Haythorn, at your service—and who do I have the pleasure of addressing?

BIRTHDAY DATE	FIRST NAME
1	Sutton
2	Drew
3	Jordan
4	Cooper
5	Ryan
6	Taylor
7	J. R.
8	Jude
9	Mo
10	Tate
11	K. C.
12	Shelby
13	Cody
14	Alex
15	Sandy
16	Cassidy
17	Quinn
18	River
19	Sawyer
20	Maverick
21	Lane
22	Shiloh
23	Riley
24	Ace
25	Dakota
26	Ash
27	Cameron
28	Blaze
29	Clay
30	Wiley
31	Colby

BIRTHDAY MONTH	LAST NAME
January	Moore
February	Shaw
March	Haythorn
April	Kent
May	McRae
June	Welch
July	Miller
August	Mitchell
September	Gonzalez
October	Johnson
November	Smith
December	Good

The bawl of a steer,
To a cowboy's ear,
Is music of sweetest strain;
And the yelping notes
Of the gray coyotes
To him are a glad refrain.

And his jolly songs
Speed him along,
As he thinks of the little gal
With golden hair
Who is waiting there
At the bars of the home corral.

For a kingly crown
In the noisy town
His saddle he wouldn't change;
No life so free
As the life we see
Way out on the Yaso range.

from 'The Cowboy's Life' by James Barton Adams

GIVE ME A HOME WHERE THE BUFFALO ROAM(ED)

There were an estimated 60 million American bison, known colloquially as buffalo, roaming the Great Plains of America before the 1870s, but by the end of the 1880s they had been slaughtered to the point of near extinction by settlers and tourists. For thousands of years before this, bison had been a vital and sustainable source of food, clothing, and tools for Native Americans, and their loss caused deep spiritual pain. In the words of Chief Plenty Coups, of the Crow tribe, 'When the buffalo went away, the hearts of my people fell to the ground, and they could not lift them up again. After this nothing happened. There was little singing anywhere.'

Having plummeted to around 100 animals in the 1880s, bison were then protected and bred in six separate herds, and a count in 2017 recorded around 500,000 of them. The bison's near-extermination is a profound example of the consequences of over-exploiting an animal population. It's a lesson we should still be learning.

THE END OF THE 'WILD WEST'

Many factors led to the end of the cowboy heyday of the Wild West. One of these was the invention of barbed wire, which was patented in 1874 by Joseph F. Glidden of DeKalb, Illinois, and soon spread across the country.

'COWBOYS ARE BORN, NOT MADE. THEIR STORIES ARE TRUE, EVEN WHEN THEY'RE NOT.'

BAXTER BLACK

When livestock were enclosed instead of roaming free, and when it was no longer practical to drive herds across wide territories due to all the barbed-wire boundaries in the way, the era of the cowboy was dealt a severe blow.

Another factor was the expansion of coast-to-coast railway lines toward the end of the nineteenth century, which reduced the necessity for long cattle drives, and the rise of the car in the early twentieth century, which displaced horses as the primary mode of transport in towns and cities.

Other dates in the history of the end of the Old West are:

- 1883, when William F. Cody started touring his *Buffalo Bill Wild West* show, lifting lived history into the realm of entertainment;

- 1890, when the Western Frontier—the line that marked the border between the incorporated states of the US and the unsettled territories of the West—was officially closed;

- 1912, when all of New Mexico and Arizona became the 47th and 48th states respectively, meaning that there were no remaining unsettled territories on the contiguous landmass of the United States.

COWBOYS TODAY

Although the historical version of the Wild West is long past, there are still a significant number of cowboys working in the cattle trade today, all across the western US and beyond. Their responsibility is to care for their livestock from birth all the way to the cattle market, and they work in all settings, ranging from small family-owned ranches to operations covering millions of acres.

One thing that hasn't changed since the earliest cowboy days is just how hard the men and women of the ranches have to work. Although the scenery is often stunning, with no signs of manmade structures in sight, the hours are long and the weather conditions can be unrelentingly hot, cold, windy, or snowy, depending on the time of year.

It takes a tough person to be a cowboy, someone strong, self-reliant, adaptable, and resilient. Perhaps that's why the cowboy has become such an iconic figure all over the world.

DUDE, WHERE'S MY COWBOY VACAY?

As long as there have been cattle ranches, there have been tourists who wanted to get a taste of cowboy life—and when Wild West shows started touring the US and beyond in the 1880s, the demand became even greater. Enterprising cattle ranchers, from the middle of the nineteenth century onward, welcomed city folk from the East—known as 'dudes'—to come and experience ranch life, with horse riding, campfire cookouts, fishing, and other outdoor adventures.

Today's dude ranches offer an even wider range of activities, from birdwatching to yoga, and accommodation running the gamut from basic bunkhouses to luxury cabins. It's easy to see how attractive this kind of holiday has always been to worn-out city slickers and tired townsfolk. Riding down a dusty trail and navigating by the stars or fighting to reach inbox zero and negotiating for the last free meeting room? I know which challenge I would rather take on.

Grand Canyon National Park, Arizona: Perhaps the most famous landscape in the US, this enormous canyon displays an astonishing two billion years of geological history, and welcomes about five million visitors every year.

Tombstone, Arizona: A once-lawless town that was the site of the Gunfight at the O.K. Corral in 1881. It now hosts several museums and even offers live shoot-out reenactments!

Lone Pine, California: This town has its very own museum of film history, which is hardly surprising as over 150 Westerns were filmed in the nearby Alabama Hills, including *The Lone Ranger* and *How the West Was Won*.

Dodge City, Kansas: The 'Cowboy Capital' and a major cattle destination in the late nineteenth century, thanks to its connection to the Santa Fe Railroad.

Amarillo, Texas: Established in 1887 and named after the yellow-colored earth of the banks of the Amarillo River, this town is now the site of several rodeos and the annual Polk Street Cattle Drive.

Cody, Wyoming: Founded by its namesake, 'Buffalo Bill' Cody, in 1896, and located 52 miles east of Yellowstone National Park, Cody is home to many museums, including five that are affiliated with the Smithsonian. It also hosts the Cody Stampede Rodeo and the Cody Nite Rodeo, running nightly from June to August every year.

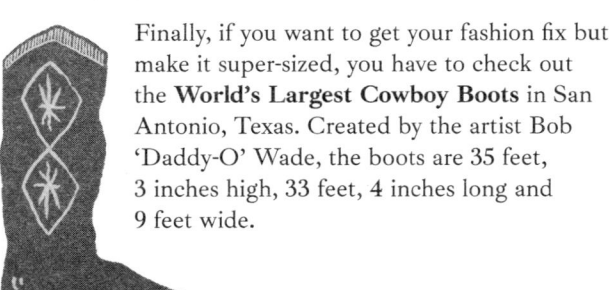

Finally, if you want to get your fashion fix but make it super-sized, you have to check out the **World's Largest Cowboy Boots** in San Antonio, Texas. Created by the artist Bob 'Daddy-O' Wade, the boots are 35 feet, 3 inches high, 33 feet, 4 inches long and 9 feet wide.

'IN THE GRAND CANYON, ARIZONA HAS A NATURAL WONDER WHICH, SO FAR AS I KNOW, IS, IN KIND, ABSOLUTELY UNPARALLELED THROUGHOUT THE REST OF THE WORLD.'

THEODORE ROOSEVELT

ACTIVITY

PLAN YOUR VERY OWN COWBOY ODYSSEY

If your feet are itchin' to move and you've a hankerin' to travel, check out some of these destinations where the cowboy life is a-waitin' to greet you. Even if you're not ready to hop on a plane just yet, you can give yourself a virtual visit with Google Earth and YouTube (and your carbon footprint will thank you for it).

WHAT'S IN A NICKNAME?

Sound like a local by using these nicknames for some key cowboy states.

Arizona	Grand Canyon State
California	Golden State
Colorado	Centennial State
Idaho	Gem State
Kansas	Sunflower State
Montana	Treasure State; Big Sky Country
Nebraska	Cornhusker State

Nevada	Silver State; Sagebrush State
New Mexico	Land of Enchantment; Land of Sunshine
North Dakota	Flickertail State; Peace Garden State
Oklahoma	Sooner State
Oregon	Beaver State
South Dakota	Coyote State; Mount Rushmore State
Texas	Lone Star State
Utah	Beehive State; Crossroads of the West
Wyoming	Cowboy State; Equality State

The history of cowboys is richly layered and complex, with people from many backgrounds coming together to work hard and build a life to be proud of. On this whistlestop tour we've only had time to see an outline of the places and pressures that created the cowboy world we know today, and there's lots more to explore.

Understanding history is how we learn to create a future that works for all of us, and knowing where the trail started can help us to map our way forward. Listening to stories from the past, especially from voices that have been overshadowed, is a great way to know more about the world and to dream about how we want it to be in the future. Enjoy the ride and grab every opportunity you can to get to know your fellow travelers, including the ones who have ridden the trail before you.

'HONOR IS LIKE A BRAND ON A COWBOY'S SOUL— ONCE BURNED IN, IT NEVER FADES.'

COWBOY SAYING

The Cowboy Code

THE TRUE CODE OF THE WEST

Back in the days of the Wild West, laws existed but there were few officials around to enforce them. A cowboy out on the trail would have to rely on his own common sense and good judgment to get his cattle safely to their destination, avoiding danger and trouble as far as possible—and being ready to meet it head-on when required.

In a setting where anything could happen, it made sense for cowboys and other travelers to follow some broad principles of behavior, which became known as 'the code of the West.' These rules are not printed in any book of law, but all true cowboys know them, and follow them.

THE BASICS

At heart, the cowboy code is based on fair play and honest dealing. If you make a promise you must do your best to keep it, no matter how many obstacles crop up along the way. When you are looking after a herd of valuable cattle, it's down to you and your team to get them safely to the end of their journey—and if that means you have to stay awake all night to guard them, then you'd best brew yourself a strong cup of coffee and get up in that saddle till dawn breaks.

A MAN AND HIS HORSE

Without his horse, a cowboy is earthbound and vulnerable, unable to cover any distances and at risk of exposure in the harsh hot or cold conditions of the landscape he's traveling through. As a result, the cowboy code has plenty to say about horses. You must never borrow a horse without permission, and you mustn't whip or kick a borrowed horse. (Obviously, you shouldn't do this to your own horse either!)

In the Wild West, horse theft was often punished quickly and harshly, and the punishment for the crime could be a swift execution—after all, losing your horse could mean death, and therefore taking a horse unlawfully could lead a thief to the same fate. Far better to respect each other's property, not just out of goodwill but to preserve your own life and health.

'A COWBOY'S WORD IS AS STRONG AS HIS ROPE—NEVER LET IT FRAY.'

COWBOY SAYING

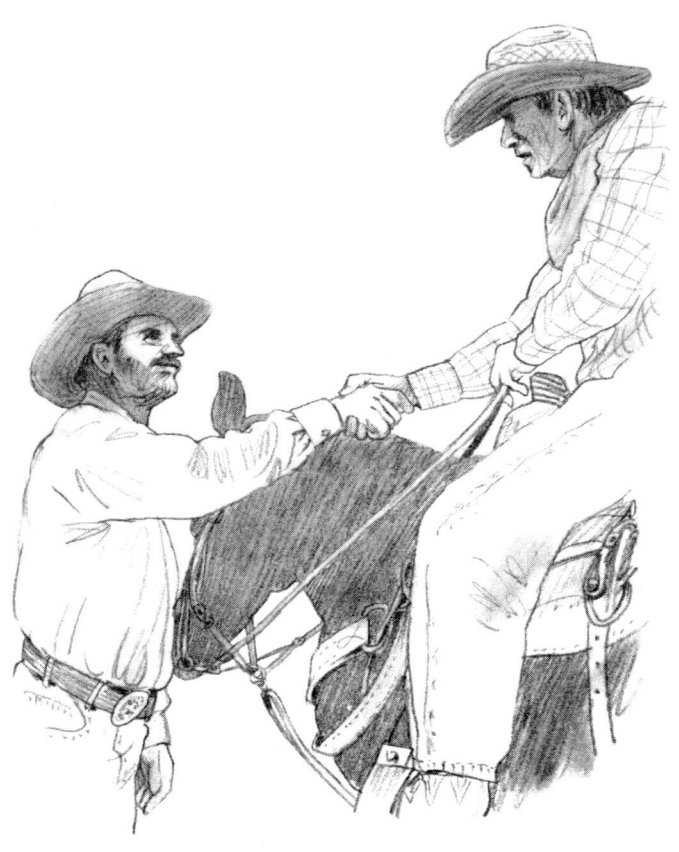

When out on horseback, if you meet another rider headed your way, the cowboy code says that you should greet each other with a friendly word and a nod, but without waving your hand—you don't want to risk spooking the other rider's horse with an unexpected gesture. If one rider dismounts, the other should too, so that both are on an equal footing.

A COWBOY AT HOME

The cowboy code applies at home as well as out on the trail, and it continues the theme of respecting the spaces you share with other people. A polite cowboy takes off his spurs inside, to protect the floor, and removes his hat as well.

If you're part of a team of cowboys and the food is ready when you get home to the bunkhouse, surprisingly, you shouldn't wait for the others to show up before you tuck in. Instead, to avoid causing delays when the latecomers arrive, you should take your plate of food and make space for them to get theirs in their turn. However, if you're at a family dinner or a party that's outside the cattle-wrangling world, it's probably wise to wait until everyone has assembled before you fill your plate. Some cowboy rules are just for cowboys!

MANAGING THE HERD

When it comes to cattle, the cowboy code becomes somewhat flexible, depending on whose cattle it's being applied to. Ownership of cattle, as shown by brand marks, should be respected, but if an enterprising cowboy finds some unmarked young 'uns or mavericks and he marks them with his own ranch's brand, he might see that as just the way the game is played. Likewise, a good cattleman erects fences to keep their cattle safely on their land, but they might also think it only reasonable to cut another ranch's fences in order to get where they need to go, or to access fresh water. When nobody's watching, the code is sometimes whatever a cowboy wants it to be. As a popular cowboy saying goes, 'Cowboys don't follow rules—they follow the wind and their own code.'

COWBOY ETIQUETTE

Cowboys may be rugged, plain-speaking people, but they are famous for their olde-worlde charm and politeness. Here are some of the guiding principles of cowboy etiquette:

- Always reply with 'Yes, sir' or 'Yes, ma'am' when spoken to.

- Never swear in front of a lady.

- ✪ Always tell the truth, unless you're spinning a yarn with friends around the campfire.

- ✪ Always keep your word. You don't need a written contract when you have a trustworthy handshake.

- ✪ Always provide hospitality to a passing stranger—one day you might need it in return.

- ✪ Never brag, but don't be overly humble either.

- ✪ Stick up for your friends, and be loyal to your family and your ranch.

HAT-IQUETTE

As well as taking off your hat when inside someone's home, there are some other golden rules for cowboys and their hats:

✪ Take off your hat when meeting someone for the first time. On future meetings you can tip your hat to show respect, but it's not essential.

✪ Always hold your hat by the crown, not the brim, when taking it off and putting it on. This helps to prevent accidentally damaging the brim.

✪ Never touch or try on another person's hat without their express permission.

✪ You can keep your hat on in public places such as bars and theaters, but you should remove it if you're blocking the view of the people in the row behind you.

✪ You should never place your hat on a bed. This is to avoid bad luck—even if the most likely kind of misfortune is your hat getting squashed when someone lies on it by accident.

✪ In US states that have hot summers, cowboys often switch from the classic felt hat to a straw hat between Memorial Day (the last Monday in May) and Labor Day (the first Monday in September). For formal events, even on sweltering days, a felt hat is always the smartest choice.

SALOON BAR RULES

When alcohol, guns, and strangers mix, trouble is never far away, and therefore the saloon bars of the Old West had their own rules of engagement. These aimed to ensure that while you might leave with a sore head and an empty wallet, you'd still have your life.

One golden rule of bar etiquette is that you should never be too curious about another person's surname, sticking to first names if that's all that a stranger offers. If the person you're talking to has something in their background that they want to keep to themselves, you must let them—after all, if you find out you're sitting next to a wanted man or woman, the night could end very badly for you. In this case, as in many others, ignorance is bliss.

It's good manners to offer a drink to someone next to you at a bar—and terrible manners to refuse. Just as in a British pub, the recipient of a drink should repay the favor with another round. And when talking with strangers at the bar, you should never enquire about the size of their cattle herd—it's the cowboy equivalent of asking someone how much money they have.

'OLD TIME COWBOY'

Come all you melancholy folks wherever you may be,
I'll sing you about the cowboy whose life is light and free.
He roams about the prairie, and, at night when he lies down,
His heart is as gay as the flowers in May in his bed upon
   the ground.

They're a little bit rough, I must confess, the most of them,
   at least;
But if you do not hunt a quarrel you can live with them in peace;
For if you do, you're sure to rue the day you joined their band.
They will follow you up and shoot it out with you just man
   to man.

Did you ever go to a cowboy whenever hungry and dry,
Asking for a dollar, and have him you deny?
He'll just pull out his pocket book and hand you a note,—
They are the fellows to help you whenever you are broke.

Go to their ranches and stay a while, they never ask a cent;
And when they go to town, their money is freely spent.
They walk straight up and take a drink, paying for every one,
And they never ask your pardon for anything they've done.

When they go to their dances, some dance while others pat
They ride their bucking bronchos, and wear their broad-
   brimmed hats;
With their California saddles, and their pants stuck in
   their boots,
You can hear their spurs a-jingling, and perhaps some of
   them shoots.

Come all soft-hearted tenderfeet, if you want to have some fun;
Go live among the cowboys, they'll show you how it's done.
They'll treat you like a prince, my boys, about them there's
 nothing mean;
But don't try to give them too much advice, for all of them
 ain't green.

Anon.

COWBOY ETHICS TODAY

The cowboy code gained popularity after the author Zane Grey published a novel in 1934 titled *Code of the West*, which was made into a film in 1947, and remains popular today. Wherever you hang your cowboy hat, you can fit in a poster of inspirational cowboy mottos to help you get ready to face the world while sitting upright in your saddle.

The cowboy code has even found its place in schools: in Elkhart County, Indiana, elementary school students have been participating in lessons based on its principles. Tackling tasks that require teamwork and good communication, led by a cheerful cowboy-hatted guide, children have learned to overcome the barriers between them in order to achieve a common goal. The little cowpunchers might have to wrangle a horde of unruly balloons rather than a hundred-head of cattle, but the concentration and care required to get the job done are just the same. With a little down-to-earth common sense and by working together as a team, these mini cowboys and cowgirls develop skills that will help them when they're out riding the wild lands of adult life.

GENE AUTRY'S TEN COWBOY COMMANDMENTS

The singer, actor, producer, and businessman Gene Autry (1907–1998), famous for singing hits such as 'South of the Border (Down Mexico Way)' and 'Back in the Saddle Again,' hosted a popular weekly radio show called *Gene Autry's Melody Ranch* from 1940 to 1956. Over time, he developed ten commandments that formed his 'Cowboy Code,' promoting an ethical, moral, and patriotic lifestyle that any aspiring cowboy, young or old, should follow:

1. The Cowboy must never shoot first, hit a smaller man, or take unfair advantage.

2. He must never go back on his word, or a trust confided in him.

3. He must always tell the truth.

4. He must be gentle with children, the elderly, and animals.

5. He must not advocate or possess racially or religiously intolerant ideas.

6. He must help people in distress.

7. He must be a good worker.

8. He must keep himself clean in thought, speech, action, and personal habits.

9. He must respect women, parents, and his nation's laws.

10. The Cowboy is a patriot.

Aside from the assumption that the would-be cowboy reading these rules is male, there's a lot in this list that feels evergreen today. Even without a herd to look after or a horse to ride, anyone who treats others with kindness and disavows intolerance of all kinds seems like a pretty fine model of a cowboy.

ACTIVITY

COME UP WITH YOUR OWN COWBOY CODE

Your life may not revolve around cattle-rustling, horse-trading, and bar-room bust-ups, but we all face the challenge of dealing with friends, colleagues, and strangers in the fairest way possible, while standing up for our own needs.

How could you adapt the cowboy code to suit your daily life? Here are some examples to get you started.

✪ Say what you mean and mean what you say.

✪ There's room on the prairie for everyone.

✪ Treat everyone with respect and look for the good in everyone you meet.

✪ Keep your eye on the horizon—that's where you'll find what you're looking for.

✪ Tell the truth, with kindness.

✪ Stand up against injustice, even if others criticize you for it.

- ⭐ Every day is a new opportunity.

- ⭐ Take responsibility for your decisions, and don't be afraid to make mistakes.

- ⭐ Keep going, even when others doubt you.

- ⭐ Know what matters, and let go of what doesn't.

When you've come up with your own personal guidelines, you can write them out and stick them on a noticeboard to inspire you every day—or even get an old-fashioned wooden sign printed, headed with 'In this house, we...'

Maybe by thinking through our own cowboy code, we can influence other people to see the best in each other and treat one another with kindness and respect, too. Now wouldn't that be purty!

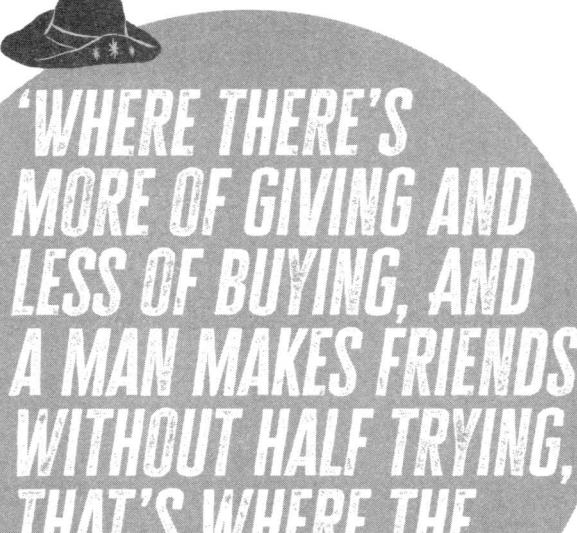

The cowboy code was developed in the wild, rugged terrain of the West, where people had to rely on their own courage and adaptability to survive dangerous journeys and risky encounters. For a lot of us today, our struggles are more likely to relate to difficult co-workers, money pressures, and broken-down trains, but those cowboy ideals of resilience and independence might be just what we need to face the day with a wry chuckle instead of a howl of rage, and to keep moving forward instead of losing hope.

By adopting our very own version of the cowboy code, perhaps we can approach life's ups and downs with the easy-going, practical grace of a true cowboy. It's worth a try, anyway!

'DESTINY IS THAT WHICH WE ARE DRAWN TOWARDS AND FATE IS THAT WHICH WE RUN INTO.'

WYATT EARP

Legends & Lore

A LAND OF LEGENDARY CHARACTERS

Thanks to its vast size and relative lack of law enforcement, the Wild West was the perfect place for outsize characters to flourish and to indulge in hair-raising antics, from horse theft and cattle rustling to bank robbery and murder. In this chapter we'll look at some of the key players from the golden age of the West—many of whom you wouldn't want to meet down an alley on a dark night, or even in the middle of the street on a sunny day.

OUTLAWS

Jesse James (1847–1882): As a young man, Jesse James and his brother Frank participated in guerrilla violence against Union soldiers in the American Civil War, and in the post-war period they robbed banks, stagecoaches, and even trains, becoming the first people in American history to rob a moving train. Painted by some as a kind of rebel folk hero, James met his end when he was shot in the head by one of his own gang members.

Belle Starr (1848–1889): Born as Myra Maybelle Shirley in Missouri, Belle Starr had a classical education and learned to play the piano. After the death of her brother in the Civil War and her family's move to Texas, she became associated with Jesse James's gang and married one of its members, Jim Reed. After Reed's death, she married Sam Starr, a Cherokee man whose family were active horse and cattle thieves and whiskey bootleggers. A sharpshooter with a fine sense of style, Starr led a life of crime with her partners, until she was shot in the back in Eufaula, Oklahoma, in a murder case that has never been solved.

John Wesley Hardin (1853–1895): Having committed his first murder at the age of 15, John Wesley Hardin went on to kill as many as 40 more before he was sent to prison at the age of 23. During the 17 years he spent behind bars, Hardin studied law, and on his release he passed the Texas State Bar exams and set up a law practice. However, his tendency to reach for the gun remained unchanged, and he died from a shot to the back of the head in El Paso's Acme Saloon in 1895.

'THEY SAY I KILLED SIX OR SEVEN MEN FOR SNORING. WELL, IT AIN'T TRUE. I ONLY KILLED ONE MAN FOR SNORING.'

JOHN WESLEY HARDIN

Billy the Kid (1859–1881): Perhaps the most famous gunslinger in the Wild West, Billy was born as Henry McCarty in New York City. On his father's death, the family moved out west, but when his mother died, her second husband abandoned him, aged just 14. He later took on the name 'William H. Bonney, Jr' and lived a life of cowboying mixed in with gambling, horse theft, and killing. He was sentenced to hang for the murder of Sheriff William Brady in New Mexico in April 1881, and escaped by pulling off an audacious jailbreak, but three months later he was ambushed and killed by another famous figure of the West, Pat Garrett, at the age of 21.

'BILLY THE KID'

I'll sing you a true song of Billy the Kid,
I'll sing of the reckless deeds that he did
Way out in New Mexico a long time ago,
When a man's only friend was his own forty-four.

When Billy the Kid was a very young lad
In old Silver City he went to the bad.
Way out in the West with a knife in his hand
At the age of twelve years he killed his first man.

Fair Mexico maidens play guitars and sing
Songs about Billy their boy bandit king.
Now here is young manhood that reached its sad end
He'd notch on his pistol for twenty-one men.

Now 'twas on the same night that poor Billy died,
He said to his friends: 'I'm not satisfied.
It's twenty-one men that I've put bullets through
And Sheriff Pat Garrett's gonna make twenty-two.'

Now this is how Billy the Kid met his fate,
The bright moon was shining and the hour was late.
Shot down by Pat Garrett who once was his friend
The poor outlaw's life had reached its sad end.

There's many a fine boy with a face fine and fair
Who starts out in life with a chance to be square,
But just like poor Billy he wanders astray
Then he loses his life in the very same way.

Traditional

Butch Cassidy (1866–1908): Another bank and train robber, Butch Cassidy was born as Robert LeRoy Parker and became famous as the leader of the 'Wild Bunch' gang. He and his equally notorious partner in crime, Harry Alonzo Longabaugh—'the Sundance Kid'—eventually fled to New York and then to South America. He either died at the hands of bandits in Bolivia in 1908, or survived and lived on under a new name—we will never know for sure.

Harry Alonzo Longabaugh, 'the Sundance Kid' (1867–1908): Having left home at 15, Harry Longabaugh took his famous nickname from a town in Wyoming where

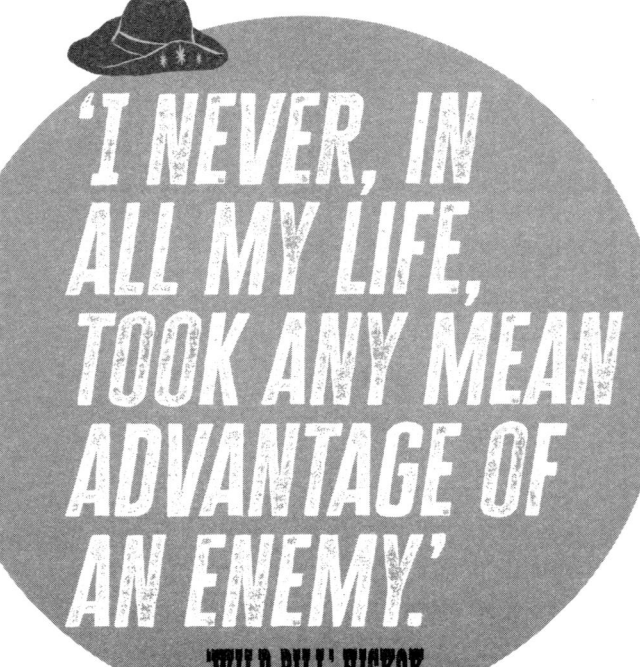

he served his first and only prison sentence, for horse theft, from August 1887 to February 1889. He teamed up with Butch Cassidy and the Wild Bunch in the closing years of the nineteenth century, and gained a reputation as the gang's fastest gunslinger and best shot. Sundance and Cassidy are remembered for their daring robberies of trains and banks, and their outlaw-hero status was consolidated by the 1969 film that bears their names.

LAW ENFORCERS

'Wild Bill' Hickok (1837–1876): James Butler 'Wild Bill' Hickok was an adventurer and gunfighter who would eventually become the marshal of Abilene, Kansas. He was ambidextrous and wore pistols on both sides of his body with the handles pointing forward, so they were ready to grab quickly with a two-handed, cross-armed draw. As a sharpshooter with a larger-than-life personality, Hickok has been frequently celebrated in films, books, and television shows.

Bass Reeves (1838–1910): Bass Reeves was born into slavery in Arkansas and managed to flee from his enslavers during the American Civil War. He lived among Native Americans in what was then called Indian Territory and later became Kansas and Oklahoma, learning the languages and customs of the Cherokee, Creek, and Seminole peoples. Later, he became a US Marshal, and

in his long career he made up to 4,000 arrests. As well as being featured in films, television series, and books, he may also have been the inspiration for the fictional character the Lone Ranger, due to his close relationship with Native Americans and his knowledge of their tracking skills.

Wyatt Earp (1848–1929): Wyatt Earp was not just one of the most famous lawmen of the Old West, he was also a gambler, con artist, and sometime saloonkeeper. His career in law enforcement began in 1870 and took him across multiple states, first as a local constable in Missouri and later as assistant marshal in Dodge City, Kansas. In 1879, he moved to Tombstone, Arizona, where his brother Virgil would become the town marshal. Then in 1881, three Earp brothers, Wyatt, Virgil, and Morgan, with their friend Doc Holliday, faced off against the Clanton Gang in the famous shoot-out at the O.K. Corral. He died at the age of 80 in 1929.

Pat Garrett (1850–1908): As a young man, Pat Garrett worked as a cowboy and buffalo hunter in Texas and New Mexico, and later became a bartender in Fort Sumner, New Mexico, where it is believed he was on friendly gambling terms with Billy the Kid, to the point where they were given the nicknames 'Big Casino' and 'Little Casino.' In 1880, Garrett was elected sheriff of Lincoln County and took on the pursuit of the Kid, finally killing him on 14 July 1881. Like so many other gunslingers of the Old West, he died at gunpoint, in a roadside dispute in New Mexico in 1908. Whether his shooting was an act of self-defence or a cold-blooded execution remains a mystery to this day.

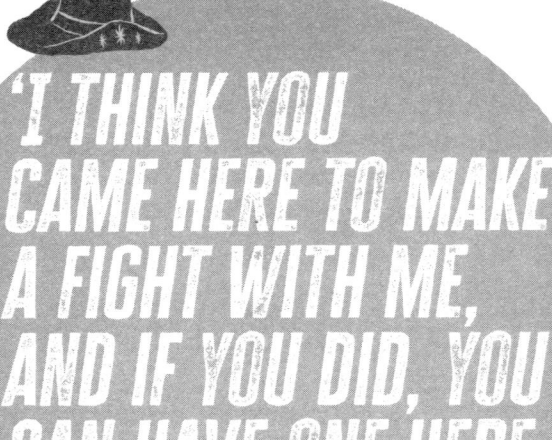

'I THINK YOU CAME HERE TO MAKE A FIGHT WITH ME, AND IF YOU DID, YOU CAN HAVE ONE HERE RIGHT NOW.'

WYATT EARP

THE LORE OF COWBOY LIFE

As well as good sense and skill, a cowboy needs a little luck to reach the end of the trail in one piece and with a full complement of cattle, horses, and teammates. In order to pack as much luck as possible, cowboys take heed of certain superstitions, because whether they're true or not, why take chances when you're out in the wild lands and far from the safety of home? Here are some of the guidelines that keep a superstitious cowboy from harm out on the trail.

- ✪ Never change a horse's name, no matter how much you may dislike it.

- ✪ When mounting a horse, always put your left foot in the stirrup first, not your right.

- ✪ Don't whistle after dark, in case you attract the attention of coyotes or supernatural entities.

- ✪ Never wear a peacock feather in your hat. (This doesn't sound like a difficult situation to avoid, as the Wild West was presumably not awash with peacocks...)

- ✪ Don't worry if you step in manure, as this will bring you good luck.

- ✪ Never accept someone else's old boots, as you will step into their troubles when you put them on.

- Never wear yellow at a rodeo, and don't compete at one with coins in your pocket, as that's all you might win.

- Never accept a knife as a gift, as it might sever your relationship with the giver. Instead, you must always 'pay' for the knife, even if you only offer a penny.

- Don't pay with a $50 bill, as this will bring you bad luck—ask for different notes if you are offered one. (In the UK, a similar superstition used to be attached to the crown coin, with people fearing they might lose their job if they accepted one.)

A COWBOY HORROR STORY

Cowboys are, by and large, pretty down-to-earth people and not easily scared. However, when you're out in the wilds, with potential dangers all around you, it's only natural that sometimes you might experience fear of the unknown, especially when you hear unexplained rustling in the sagebrush around you.

Theodore Roosevelt (1858–1919), the 26th president of the United States, recorded a tale told to him by a German cowboy in his 1893 book *Hunting the Grisly and Other Sketches*. The cowboy, 'a grisled, weather-beaten old mountain hunter, named Bauman,' was out beaver trapping with a partner, and the two of them set up camp in a wild and lonely pass. Their camp was disrupted and broken up by a creature that seemed to be about the same size as a bear, but its tracks had only two footprints—could it have been a creature that walked upright, like a human?

The next day, after a troubled night's sleep, Bauman left the camp to retrieve and prepare the beavers that their traps had caught, and when he returned to meet up with his hunting partner, a horrible sight awaited him. As Roosevelt continues:

The unfortunate man, having finished his packing, had sat down on the spruce log with his face to the fire, and his back to the dense woods, to wait for his companion. While thus waiting, his monstrous assailant, which must have been lurking nearby in the woods, waiting for a chance to catch one of the adventurers unprepared, came silently up from behind, walking with long, noiseless steps, and seemingly still on two legs. Evidently unheard, it reached the man, and broke his neck while it buried its teeth in his throat. It had not eaten the body, but apparently had romped and gambolled round it in uncouth, ferocious glee, occasionally rolling over and over it; and had then fled back into the soundless depths of the woods.

Bauman, utterly unnerved, and believing the creature was half-human or half-devil, abandoned everything but his rifle and struck off at speed down the pass, not halting until he reached the beaver meadows where the hobbled ponies were still grazing. Mounting, he rode onwards through the night, until far beyond the reach of pursuit.

ACTIVITY

TELL A SPOOKY TALE OR THREE

There's nothing to match the spine-chilling thrill of hearing a scary story face to face, told by someone you know, and if it's late and the only illumination comes from flickering candles or the glow of a campfire, then things get even spookier.

Gather a small group of friends in your darkened living room—or better yet, around a fire pit outside—and supply everyone with snacks and drinks. Then take turns telling stories to make each other's hair stand on end, diving into the scariest depths of your imaginations. A night in front of the TV could never provide such delicious terrors!

The world of the cowboy contains every kind of character, from upstanding heroes to villainous outlaws, and everyone in between. We can all choose how we're going to ride into each day: is it with outlaw energy, taking no prisoners when faced with a difficult situation, or with stand-up cowboy heroism, bearing the challenges of life with fortitude and resilience?

The truth is that we probably need a bit of both of these sets of characteristics to get through life—but ask yourself: do you want to appear on someone else's WANTED poster, or would you rather go down in history in a cowboy ballad celebrating the ways you made life better for the people you've met?

Even if you're not wearing a cowboy hat while riding a barely tamed mustang as you go about your daily life, you can still choose to be a legend, and show the world your noble bearing and fine character. It's good to celebrate the heroes all around us, too, whether they are key workers, friends and family, or even strangers that we pass on the street. Tip the brim of your cowboy hat to them as you ride by, to show you recognize them as the legends they are.

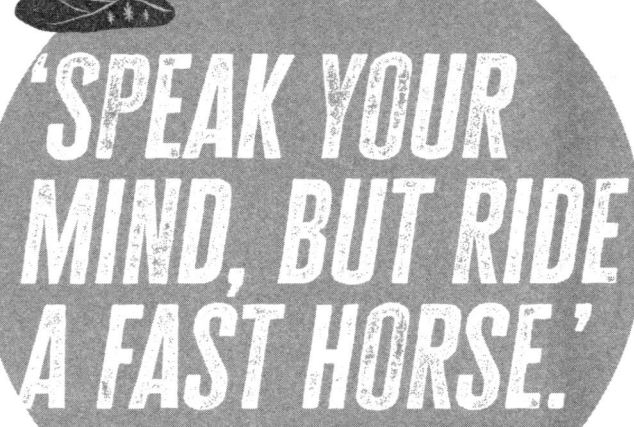

Words from the Range

COWBOY LINGO

If you've ever watched a movie or TV series about cowboys, you'll know that they have some pretty rootin'-tootin' expressions—ones that you don't hear every day when you're far from the rolling plains of the West.

Here's a mini dictionary to get you promoted from greenhorn to seasoned hand, lickety-split.

bellyaching: complaining

clip someone's horns: take someone down a peg or two

coffee boiler: someone who doesn't pull their weight, sitting around watching the coffee pot instead of working

cow chips: dry chunks of cow manure, used as fuel for fires

cow juice: milk

desert canary: donkey

dig for your cannon: reach for your gun

dogie: a motherless calf in the herd

drag man: the cowboy who brings up the rear of the herd, inevitably getting covered in dust and dirt in the process

eat gravel: fall off a horse and hit the ground

greenhorn: an inexperienced cowboy

hit the hay: go to bed

hornswoggle: cheat or swindle someone

horse feathers: utter nonsense, balderdash, lies

howdy: the cowboy way of saying 'how do you do?', or in other words, 'hi!'

jawing: talking too much

light a shuck: get out of here, make a swift exit

maverick: an unbranded calf

mustang: a wild or feral horse

nighthawk: a herder who watches over the cattle at night to keep them safe from thieves and predators

ornery: grumpy, fed up

persuader: a euphemistic name for a gun

point man: the cowboy who rides in front of the herd, setting the direction of the cattle drive

prairie strawberries: beans

ramrod: the foreman or second-in-command to the trail boss

remuda: a herd of horses belonging to a ranch

ride shank's mare: travel on foot, instead of on horseback

all roostered up: drunk

scabbard: holster

skedaddle: leave in a hurry

sweater: someone hanging around the edge of camp hoping for a free meal

tell a windy: tell an unbelievable story

waddie/waddy: a hired hand who joins the ranch in the busy season

wagon boss: the manager of a ranch's cowboys

what in tarnation?: a cowboy exclamation meaning 'what the heck?'

wrangler: the person who takes care of the horses in a cattle drive

As I walked out one morning for pleasure,
I spied a cow-puncher all riding alone;
His hat was throwed back and his spurs was a jingling,
As he approached me a-singin' this song,

Whoopee ti yi yo, git along little dogies,
It's your misfortune, and none of my own.
Whoopee ti yi yo, git along little dogies,
For you know Wyoming will be your new home.

from 'Whoopee ti yi yo, git along little dogies,' Anon.

WARDROBE WORDS

It's easy to picture a cowboy outfit, with denim jeans, a plaid shirt, and a sturdy, wide-brimmed hat to keep off the assaults of sun and rain. But there's a lot of specialized terminology behind that classic look. Here are some of the words you'll be using to get outfitted for the prairie at the general store in town.

CHAPS FOR EVERY KIND OF CHAP AND CHAPESS

Chaps are the sturdy leather leg coverings that a cowboy wears to protect their trousers from being worn away by long hours in the saddle, not to mention the thorns and other trouser-destroyers a rider might encounter on the trail. Formed as two separate legs and fastened round the waist, they don't have a seat, meaning that they are not worn without trousers underneath—or not usually, anyway.

Chaps come in different styles, each suited for different conditions:

Shotgun or stovepipe chaps are tube-shaped, and the wearer climbs into them. They are ideal for cold-weather settings, as they are effective at trapping body heat. They are often decorated with a fringe on the outer seam.

Batwing chaps are easier to put on and take off, as they fasten around the leg with buckles and are much wider than shotgun chaps. They allow the wearer to move more freely, and their wider surface area makes them perfect for decoration. You'll often see batwing chaps being worn by rodeo riders.

Woollies are, as the name suggests, covered in fleece or fur to protect cowboys riding in the coldest areas, such as the Rocky Mountains. The thick, warm covering is applied to the upper side of a pair of canvas shotgun chaps, making them flexible to wear but thick and warm on the side that faces the weather.

IF YOU WANT TO GET AHEAD... GET A HAT

It is a truth universally acknowledged that a cowboy ain't a cowboy without his or her hat—but less well known is the wide variety of hats that cowboys can choose from.

Sugar-loaf sombrero: Although today we don't tend to think of sombreros as being worn by cowboys, this style of hat, with its conical 'sugar loaf' crown and upturned brim, was a key influence on the later hats popularized by Stetson and other makers. The outlaw William H. Bonney, Jr, known as Billy the Kid, was known for wearing a sugar-loaf sombrero. This spelled out bad news for a friend of his, Charlie Bowdre, who was mistaken for the Kid while wearing a similar hat in 1880, and shot dead by the posse of Sheriff Pat Garrett.

Derby: Another surprising hat fact is that the earliest cowboys often wore a derby (pronounced to rhyme with 'Herbie') – the style that Brits would call a bowler hat. After all, this close-fitting and tough hat was developed to stay on the heads of gamekeepers in England as they rode through woodland, so it makes sense that it would offer decent protection to Americans on horseback, too.

The Boss of the Plains: The son of a hatmaker, John B. Stetson spent time traveling through Colorado and spotted a business opportunity when he realized how impractical some cowboys' hats were, made from fur, straw, or wool. In 1865 Stetson designed *that* hat that has become synonymous with his name, based on the sombrero, with a wide brim and a high crown and made from waterproof felt. Worn by stars including Calamity Jane, Will Rogers, and Tom Mix, it is the ultimate symbol of cowboy quality.

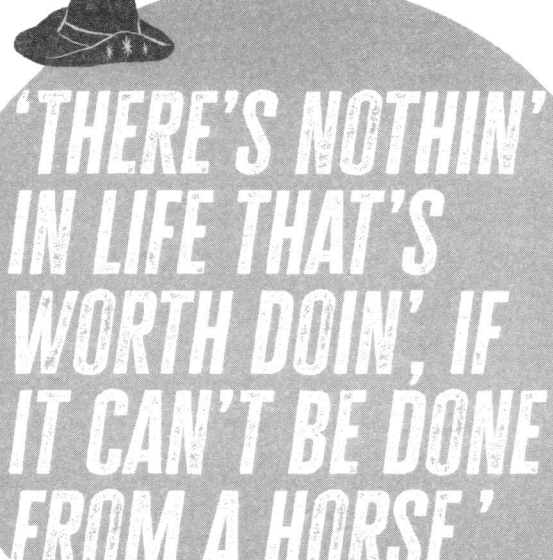

Montana peak: The Montana peak hat is a variation of the classic Boss of the Plains style, with the crown creased inward into four corners. This style has often been used in uniforms, and is famously worn by the Royal Canadian Mounted Police, or 'Mounties.'

Poet hat: It's possible you haven't heard of the 'poet hat,' but you've certainly seen it. This brown felt hat with a deep crease in the crown and a brim that sweeps down at the front and swings gently up on either side was designed especially for Harrison Ford to wear as the iconic adventurer Indiana Jones. And where was this American classic created? In London, by the Herbert Johnson brand of the House of Swaine, which first popularized the poet style in the early 1900s.

Stampede strings or **wind strings** can be attached to your inner hat band and fastened under your chin to stop your hat flying off in wild conditions.

COWBOY KIT AND CABOODLE

Here are some of the other cowboy essentials that keep the men and women of the ranch looking swell:

Bolo tie: Unlike a classic office attire tie, the bolo tie consists of a thin leather braid, usually black, with metal tips, held together at the neck with a decorated clasp. This style of tie has been designated the official tie of Arizona, New Mexico, and Texas at various points over the past fifty years.

Slicker: A waterproof coat to keep the worst of the rain off you.

Spurs: These metal additions to cowboy boots have a U-shaped curve that fits around the heel, with a piece sticking out at the back, ranging from a highly decorative, spinning, spiked wheel to a simple, smooth, round knob. They are used to communicate instructions to a horse— but they are just as popular with cowboys who never ride, to show off their cowboy style to the world.

Suspenders: Also called braces,' these are essential for keeping your trousers up.

Wrist cuffs: These wide leather bindings are tied around a cowboy's wrist to protect against injury and damage from barbed wire, kicking animals, and rope burns.

COWBOY WISDOM

With very little in the way of books, and no TV shows or social media feeds to distract them, cowboys of old had plenty of time to think when they were out on the trail. And even today, with patchy cell-phone reception and abundant natural scenery, cowboy work still offers ample opportunity for reflection on the meaning of a life well lived.

As a result, there is a rich collection of sayings that capture the down-to-earth humor of cowboy wisdom. Which of these cowboy musings means the most to you—and which one are you going to drop into your next conversation?

- ✪ 'The only thing faster than a horse is gossip in a small town.'

- ✪ 'Cowboys and men are two totally different breeds.'

- ✪ 'Letting the cat out of the bag is a whole lot easier than putting it back in.'

- ★ 'Never smack a man who's chewin' tobacco.'

- ★ 'Never drink unless you're alone or with somebody.'

- ★ 'Good judgement comes from experience, and a lot of that comes from bad judgement.'

- ★ 'Don't squat with your spurs on.'

- ★ 'Never ask a barber if he thinks you need a haircut.'

- ★ 'Always drink upstream from the herd.'

- ★ 'When in doubt, let your horse do the thinking.'

- ★ 'Just because trouble comes visiting doesn't mean you have to offer it a seat.'

- ★ 'Never approach a bull from the front, a horse from the rear, or a fool from any direction.'

- ★ 'If you're riding ahead of the herd, take a look back every now and then to make sure it's still there.'

- ★ 'Never miss a good chance to shut up.'

COWBOY INSULTS

It's not just in the field of good advice that cowboy language finds a chance to shine, of course. Being a cowboy involves working with people who are highly skilled and trustworthy—and sometimes with people who are the polar opposite of those qualities. So it's not surprising that cowpokes have some richly expressive ways of describing people who let the side down. Do you know anyone who deserves these descriptions?

Someone is so stupid that...

- They couldn't hit the floor if they fell out of bed.

- They couldn't teach a hen to cluck.

- If they were bacon they wouldn't even sizzle.

- If you put their brains in a bumblebee it'd fly backward.

Someone is so tone deaf that...

- They couldn't carry a tune in a bucket.

Someone is so crooked that...

- You can't tell from their tracks if they're coming or going.

Someone is so low that...

✪ They could sit on a cigarette paper and hang their feet over the edge.

Someone is so mean that...

✪ They wouldn't give you a case of measles.

Someone is so arrogant that...

✪ They think the sun comes up just to hear them crow.

Someone is so useless that...

✪ They're as handy as hip pockets on a hog.

Finally, if you meet someone who brags all the time but never shows anything to prove it, you can issue the ultimate cowboy putdown, by saying that they are 'all hat and no cattle.'

ACTIVITY

COWBOY COMPARISONS

Add a bit of cowboy charm to your life by mixing any of these phrases into your daily conversations. Whether you're in a board meeting or going out with someone for that all-important first date, these comparisons are sure to make you as popular as a coffee pot by a campfire!

I'm / He's / She's / They're / We're / It's...

As welcome as a rattlesnake at a square dance.	As happy as a clam at high tide.	As frisky as a colt.
As cold as a beaver's belly.	As busy as a bobtail steer brushing flies.	As brave as a dog that ain't met a porcupine yet.
As fetching as a bowl of butter beans.	As dark as the inside of a cow.	As country as a baked bean sandwich.
As wild as a bronc with a burr in his tail.	As scared as a sinner in a cyclone.	As weak as a worn-out flea.

There's more to being a cowboy than using the right words, but if you take on some of the catchphrases and idioms of the men and women who roam the West, protecting their cattle and facing down danger with bravery and good humor, maybe some of those cowboy qualities will rub off on you, too. And you're certain to raise a smile when you give your bicycle a brisk instruction to giddy-up or tell your friends at work that seeing them makes you as happy as a dog with two tails.

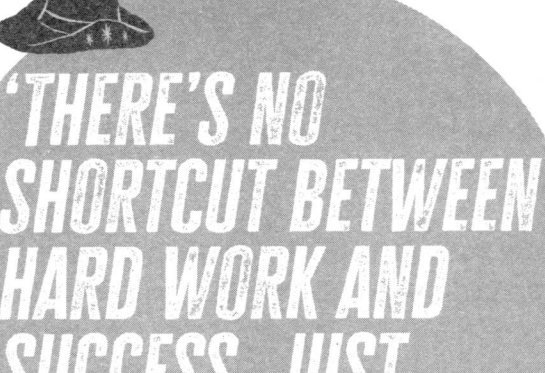

Ranch Lessons

NOT FOR THE FAINT-HEARTED—THE REALITY OF RANCH LIFE

One classic image of a cowboy home is the Dutton ranch in the television series *Yellowstone*, with its stone-built mansion and spacious farm buildings. However, for the earliest cattle ranchers, home was often a structure built with whatever materials could be found, and the biggest challenge was to keep out the excesses of heat, cold, wind, rain, and snow. And even today, small family ranches are unlikely to be luxurious; instead, they are places where everyone works hard throughout the year to keep the business going.

It would take a lifetime to learn the knowledge and skills required to run a ranch, but in this chapter we're going to corral a few key facts and lessons that will help you decide if ranch life is for you!

WANTED: EARLY BIRDS

If you're like me and you appreciate a long lie-in whenever possible, then life on a ranch might come as rather a rude awakening, in the most literal sense. A cowboy's primary duty is to look after his or her animals, and a typical first task of the day is to feed and groom the horses and check that they are healthy and ready for the day's work. In ranches where the horses roam free, you'll also have to gather them in before you can do any of this. And obviously this all takes place before you can even think about having your own breakfast. When the horses have been checked, brushed, and fed, then you can head back to the farmhouse for your own refueling. After that, the rest of the day's work can begin!

HORSE CODE

Without horses, there would be no cowboys—just imagine being on two feet and trying to keep up with a herd of cattle, or trying to round up an animal who has strayed from the herd and got lost. A horse is a cowboy's most vital tool, but more important than that, his or her most constant companion throughout the working day.

Cowboys have their own language when it comes to horses—here's some horsey vocabulary to get you up to speed in the stables and beyond:

bangtail: a wild horse, also known as a mustang

boss mare: an older female horse with plenty of common sense

bronco or bronc: a horse that has not been broken to accept a saddle or harness

buckskin: a tan-colored horse with a black tail

claybank: dun-colored; a yellow-gray coat with black mane and tail

cow sense: a horse's ability to work on cow-related tasks such as roping

glass-eyed: a horse with blue or white eyes

hay burner: a horse that eats a lot of hay but doesn't earn its keep through work

high binder: a horse with a vicious temperament

mustang: a wild or feral horse

outlaw: an untameable horse

owl-headed: a horse that turns its head to look around a lot

puddin'-foot: an awkward horse

snuffy: a wild, high-spirited horse

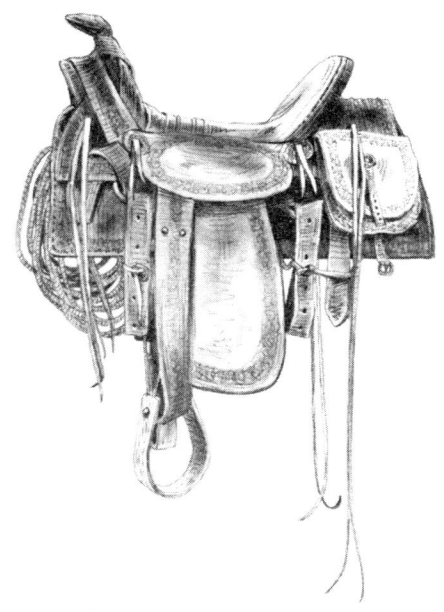

BACK IN THE SADDLE

You might think that nothing should ever come between a cowboy and his or her horse, but there is of course one vital thing that must do this: a saddle. This piece of equipment is essential for keeping the rider safely in place and the horse comfortable, and allowing both to travel for tens of miles in a single day's work without injury or exhaustion. In the late nineteenth century a fully

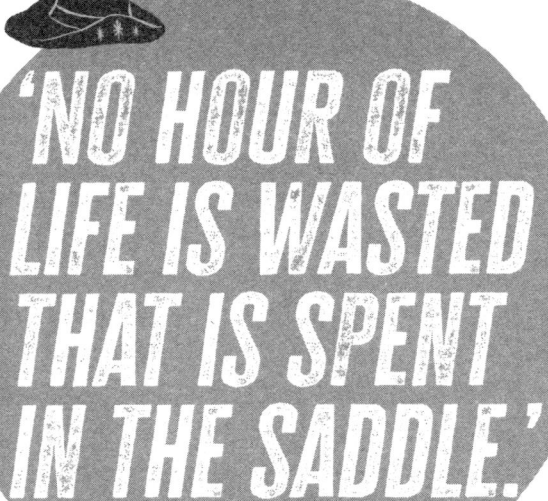

rigged-out saddle could cost around $30, or one month of a cowboy's pay, but if properly looked after, it could last up to 30 years. The saddle was such an important part of a cowboy's life that the phrase 'to hang up your saddle' has come to mean 'to retire'—as that's the only reason a cowboy wouldn't need their saddle anymore.

ANATOMY OF A SADDLE

A saddle is made up of several different pieces, which all serve specific functions. The foundational part of a saddle is the **saddle tree**, a framework made from wood or synthetic materials that spreads the weight of the rider evenly across the horse's back. A **skirt**, usually made of leather, covers the saddle tree and gives extra form and stability to the saddle. At the front of the saddle is the **pommel**, which rises up in front of the rider. This is where the **saddle horn** is attached—a useful anchoring point for attaching a rope, or just for holding onto for a little extra stability. The **seat** itself sits behind the pommel, and this is followed by the **cantle**, a slightly curved section that rises up behind the rider, giving them extra support.

Two wide leather **fenders** dangle down the sides of the horse, connecting the **stirrups** to the saddle, and the saddle itself is secured to the horse with two leather **cinches**—a front cinch that goes just behind the horse's front legs, and a back cinch that stabilizes the saddle and stops it bouncing up and down on the horse's back.

RANCHES AND THEIR BRAND MARKS

People sometimes use the words 'ranch' and 'farm' interchangeably, but there is a key difference: a farm produces goods from the land, either by growing crops or raising livestock, but a ranch is a specific kind of farm that focuses entirely on livestock. Usually these are cattle or sheep, but ranches can also raise other animals, such as elk, horses, alpacas, and emus.

The practice of branding cattle by marking their skin with a hot iron goes back thousands of years, all the way back to the Ancient Egyptians, and it arrived in the Americas in the sixteenth century with the Spanish explorers, who brought cattle with them from Europe. Although ear tags are now commonly used by cattle ranchers, branding is still a very common activity, partly for its cultural aspects but also because ear tags can be lost by an adventurous animal, and they can also be removed by a rustler more easily than a brand can be altered or erased.

BRAND VALUES

Learning to read a brand is a vital skill for a cowboy out on the trail, as rounding up cattle and working out who they belong to is a key activity, especially in the spring and fall round-ups. Evans Coleman, an Arizona cowboy who wrote about pioneer life in the decades around the turn of the twentieth century, once noted that a good cowboy could understand 'the Constitution of the United States were it written with a branding iron on the side of a cow.'

Brands are usually located on a cow's hip, rib, or shoulder, with any correction being added as a smaller brand on the jaw, if necessary. Cowboys would sometimes add other marks with a knife, such as notches on the ear, wattle, or dewlap (the soft part that dangles from a cow's neck), to the point where an animal could resemble a walking billboard.

HOW TO READ A BRAND

Brands need to be simple—after all, you can't burn a whole thesaurus into a cow's hide—but also unique, and this has led ranchers over the years to become very inventive with the characters they use on their herds. Each brand consists of a combination of letters, numbers, geometric characters, and pictographs. Letters and numbers can appear in their standard form, or they can be flipped, reversed, and tilted, and they can also have details added to them such as wings or hooks.

Brands are read from left to right, from top to bottom, and from outside to inside. Here are a few of the branding variations you might see out on the range:

LETTER-BASED BRANDS

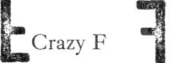 Crazy F    Reverse F    Crazy Reverse F    Tumbling F

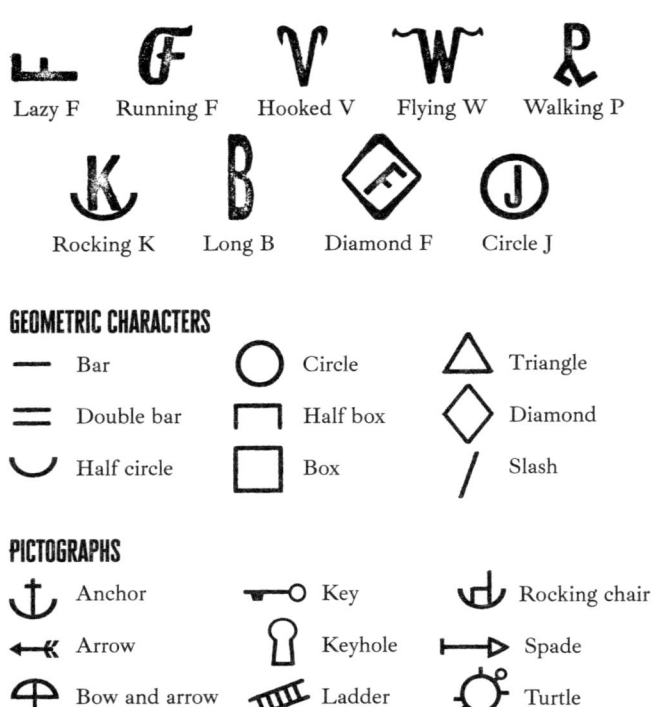

Different elements can be combined in a brand. For example, the iconic fictional brand of the Dutton ranch in the television series *Yellowstone* is a **hooked rocking Y**—or in other words, a Y with little hooks on the top and a curve underneath like a rocking horse.

CREATE YOUR OWN BRAND

Having a strong personal brand is supposed to be very important these days, but how many people can say they've developed an *actual* brand? Well, today is your day to change all that.

Roll the dice to find out what your very own cattle ranch brand will be:

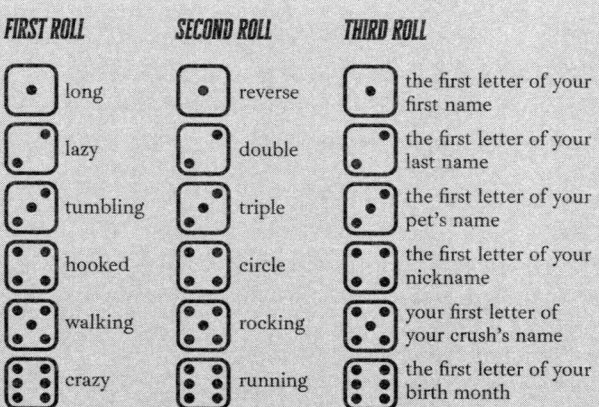

If you're feeling artistic, mock up your new brand in pen and ink or on your computer, then add it to all your online profiles—it's the original cowboy monogram!

FOR THE ROPE OF IT ALL

Another key piece of cowboy equipment is the lasso, also known as a lariat. Famed from every classic cowboy movie, lassos are used to catch animals when they stray from the main herd or when they need to be separated out from the pack so they can be tied down and branded or given medical care such as vaccination.

A lasso is typically made from twisted grass or braided rawhide (untreated cattle leather), and it has a sliding looped knot at the end known as a honda knot, which enables it to be formed into a throwing loop. A cowboy will hold the throwing loop in his or her dominant hand, with the rest of the rope held in a loose coil in his or her other hand, along with the horse's reins. More rope can be released from the non-dominant hand when it's time to throw the rope, and the cowboy can use their saddle horn as a securing point once a cow has been captured. If you loop the rope around your saddle horn a few times, so it can be easily released, this is called dallying. In rockier and rougher terrain, when there's a risk of the rope working itself free of the saddle horn, a figure-of-eight knot is used to give greater security.

If you want to rope a cow, there are two main lassoing maneuvers you'll need to master: the head catch and the heel catch. And whichever role you're taking, you'll need a cowboy companion to help you with the other one. The

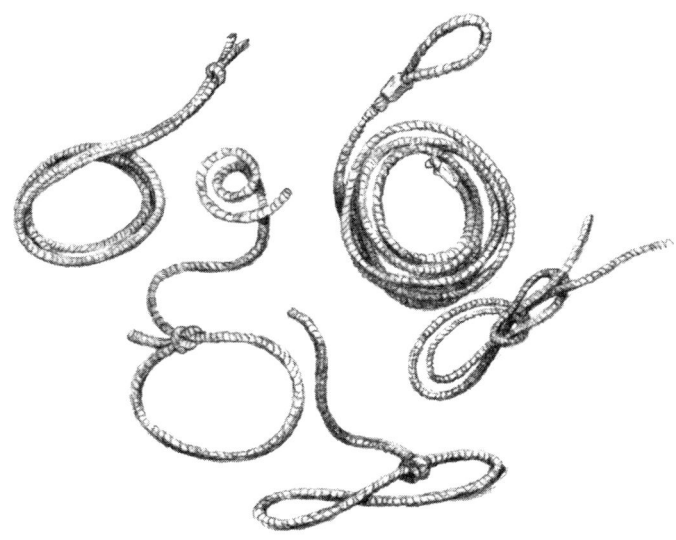

head catch involves swinging the lasso so it lands neatly over the cow's horns and pulling it tight. Then the other cowboy will throw their lasso around the cow's two back legs, using an underarm throw. The cowboy in charge of the cow's head walks their horse forward slowly, and the cowboy on the leg rope stays still, causing the cow to topple over. Once it is flat out on the ground, other cowboys can move in to brand the cow or do whatever else is necessary—or if the team is a small one, the roping cowboys can jump down and do the work while their horses hold the ropes taut.

GETTING THE COWBOY LOOK

Adding a touch of cowboy style has always been a popular fashion choice. But what does a real cowboy actually need in his or her wardrobe?

First, a reliable and well-made pair of cowboy boots. The unique design of a cowboy boot is entirely functional: the tall upper part protects the wearer's legs from being scratched by undergrowth or bitten by snakes, and the stitched embroidery adds strength, as well as style. The classic pointed toe slides into and out of a stirrup easily (although rounded and squared-off toe styles are common nowadays, too), and the distinctive underslung heel shape locks into place firmly on a stirrup without slipping through.

When it comes to clothes, you'll need a cotton button-up shirt, a sturdy pair of jeans—you may need them cut a little longer than usual, as they'll ride up when you're in the saddle—and a light jacket to keep the wind off you. For more extreme weather, add a duster (a long coat made of canvas or linen) or a slicker (a long coat made of waterproof material, for rainy and snowy conditions).

To protect your trousers, a pair of chaps is a good addition. To keep the wind from whistling down your shirt, tie on a bandana.

Finally, add a little extra pizazz with an embroidered leather belt, and top the whole outfit with a cowboy hat made of classic felt, or from straw for a summery look.

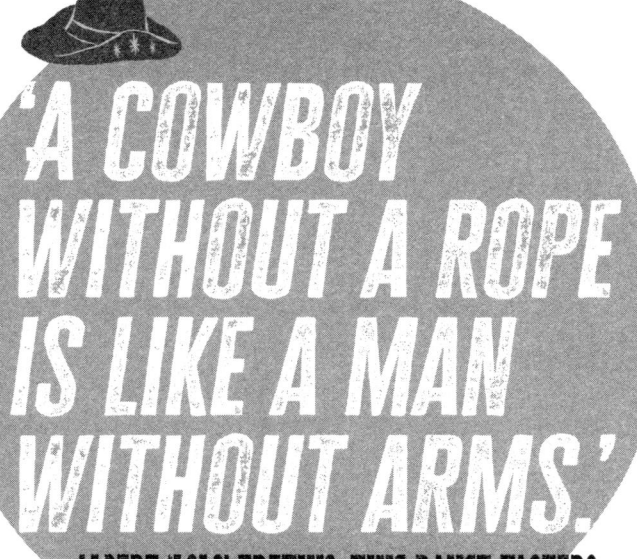

ACTIVITY

HIT THE COWBOY CATWALK EVERY DAY

Even if it's a rainy Monday and your calendar is packed with meetings rather than rodeo appearances, you can still head out the door in style and show the world your cowboy couture.

A cowboy hat will protect you from sunburn or a rain soaking, whether you're roaming an unmarked trail or a city street, and cowboy boots will keep your feet dry and comfortable in all weathers. A leather belt with an ornate buckle will not only hold your trousers up but can also display an image that captures your vibe for the day, such as a proud eagle, a majestic elk, or a wild rambling rose.

However you choose to strut your cowboy stuff, you'll be sure to draw some admiring glances, and who knows, you may inspire others to join you on your fashion journey!

If you want to become a cowboy there will be lots to learn, and it can be daunting, but every cowboy had to start somewhere. Some people start their cowboy journey as little children growing up on a farm or ranch, but others join the cowboy trail from towns and cities, and there's no age limit to when you can begin expanding your knowledge.

Whether you're planning to join a pony trek, go out on a camping odyssey, or simply hit the road for your morning commute, you can express your cowboy values through your fashion choices, showing everyone that you're a proud cowpoke who isn't afraid to stand up for what's right and who's always ready for a new adventure.

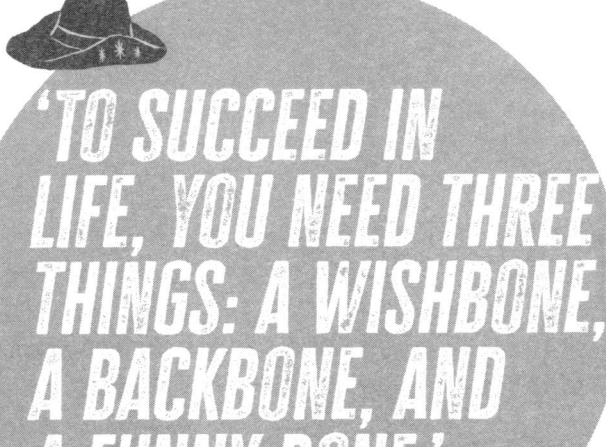

6

Stoic in the Saddle

THE HOME OF THE BRAVE

The cowboy life may have been full of adventure, but you had to be tough to endure it. An anonymous poet summed up some of the hardships of life on the trail in the 1920s in the collection *Cowboy Songs and Other Frontier Ballads* (see page 135):

The cowboy's life is a dreary, dreary life,
He's driven through the heat and cold;
While the rich man's a-sleeping on his velvet couch,
Dreaming of his silver and gold.

Spring-time sets in, double trouble will begin,
The weather is so fierce and cold;
Clothes are wet and frozen to our necks,
The cattle we can scarcely hold.

The cowboy's life is a dreary one,
He works all day to the setting of the sun;
And then his day's work is not done,
For there's his night herd to go on.

The wolves and owls with their terrifying howls
Will disturb us in our midnight dream,
As we lie on our slickers on a cold, rainy night
Way over on the Pecos stream.

from 'The Dreary, Dreary Life,' Anon.

Today's cowboys need to be just as strong and resilient, even though they now have better equipment and more high-tech tools to help them on their journeys. The hours are long, and the work is physically demanding. When it's time to rope a cow for branding, teamwork and skill are needed to ensure nobody gets hurt—but injury is always a risk for a cowboy, and it could be a long and bumpy ride home before proper treatment is available. With such demanding conditions, stoicism is a key trait of a successful cowboy, and it's one that we all need from time to time, even if the dangers on our own daily trails are not quite as severe as being kicked by a steer or bitten by a rattlesnake.

STOICISM FOR BEGINNERS

The roots of stoicism stretch back a long, long way from the open lands of the Wild West, all the way to a Greek philosopher called Zeno of Citium, who lived from *c.*334 to *c.*262 BCE. Zeno used to teach his followers in Athens in a painted colonnade, or *Stoa Poikil'*, and this location gave its name to the school of stoicism that he founded.

Stoicism teaches the importance of four key virtues:

1. Courage
2. Temperance
3. Justice
4. Wisdom

While we may sometimes associate the word 'stoic' with someone who suppresses their emotional reactions, in fact true stoics accept that life is full of ups and downs, and they call on their inner strength to cope with them with perseverance and calmness.

In the words of another stoic philosopher, Seneca the Younger (*c.* 4 BCE–*c.* 65 CE), 'To bear trials with a calm mind robs misfortune of its strength and burden.' And given that life can be generous with its misfortunes, stoicism might offer a useful approach to the challenges we face on the trail.

HAPPY COWBOY CAMPING

Have you ever tried cowboy camping? It's a lot like the traditional summer-holiday type of camping, with one key difference: you don't use a tent. Instead of getting busy with guy ropes and tent pegs, the cowboy camper spreads out his or her groundsheet, places a sleeping pad on top of it, then lies down in a sleeping bag under the stars. The advantages of this method of camping are that you have a lot less equipment to carry, and it's much quicker to set up your campsite and pack everything up the next morning. You can also enjoy your very own planetarium all night long, and easily chat with your fellow campers, without any canvas getting in the way.

Of course, cowboy camping will call on your reserves of stoicism, as you have less protection from the elements, and no barrier between your skin and any hungry mosquitos who happen to be in the area. But despite these challenges, many adventurers see cowboy camping as the best kind of camping, as you have more freedom, and you're never woken by your canvas walls rattling in the wind or by getting tangled up in your bedding in the cramped, enclosed space of a tent.

If you'd like to try a spot of cowboy camping, here are some guidelines to ensure you have a happy experience:

- Do your research before you go: check the weather forecast and the lie of the land ahead of you, and pack all the equipment you'll need to keep warm or cool.

- Pick a camping location that's not too close to a water source. This will help you to avoid being bitten by mosquitos and other winged troublemakers. A site with a strong breeze will also help to discourage clouds of insects, as they prefer stiller air.

- Pack a waterproof groundsheet that's big enough to hold both you and all your stuff – you don't want to wake up and find your backpack has soaked up the ground's dampness. Before you lay out your groundsheet, clear the surface beneath it of anything sharp or prickly, to ensure a restful night.

★ Bring a sleeping bag that you love sleeping in. You can try it out at home and make sure you find it really comfortable, so that it's not an unexpectedly new sensation when you climb into it after a hard day's hiking.

★ Keep your campsite clean and tidy, with any food packed securely away. This will help to make sure that any passing animals are less tempted to come sniffing around you during the night.

★ Finally, take a small tent or shelter with you. Although you may not need it, if a storm blows up in the night you'll be glad of the extra protection that a small pop-up tent will offer you.

LIVING WELL IN COWBOY COUNTRY

You have to rely on your wits and your knowledge of the natural world if you're going to make the most of cowboy life—and sometimes this knowledge could be the difference between life and death. Before riding out on a work mission or an adventure trail, you'll need to brush up your outdoor living skills.

FINDING WATER

Drinking water in the wild always carries some risk, as it could contain harmful microbes and parasites, so it's best to carry a portable water filter or boil for at least 1 minute any water you plan to drink. At altitudes of over 6,560 feet, the boiling time should be increased to 3 minutes. Other tactics used by old-time cowboys were never to drink from a water source that has dead animals nearby, or downstream from a place where cattle have been drinking and standing. They also preferred moving water to stagnant water, and would try to find the source of a spring or stream wherever possible, as that is always the least polluted.

BUILDING A FIRE

Safety is the number one priority whenever you are thinking about using fire in the wild. You don't want to be responsible for starting a fire that can't be controlled, so it's vital to follow some basic safety precautions. First, you need to choose a site on bare earth or rock, with no grass, trees, or other plants nearby. Your next step is to create a bed for your fire by gathering earth and building it into a layer about 4 inches deep.

To build your fire, you need tinder, kindling, and fuel wood. Tinder is the material that burns the fastest, such as dry leaves, and you use this to light the fire. Kindling is made from twigs and small sticks and is used to help the fire become established. Finally, the bigger fuel of wood branches burn slowly, allowing the fire to stay lit as long as you need it.

Keep a bucket of water close to the fire so that you can extinguish it quickly if you need to. When you want to put out the fire, sprinkle it with water until you are sure that it has been completely extinguished. You can also use sand for this purpose. Never leave a fire site until you are certain all the heat has gone—and never leave a burning fire unattended.

FORECASTING THE WEATHER

If you have a weather app on your phone and a decent amount of signal, you'll be able to read a detailed weather forecast for the terrain you're traveling through, but if you're in an internet dead-zone, then one of these traditional weather sayings might give you some useful information on what's coming:

- ✪ **'Halo around the sun or moon, rain or snow comes very soon.'** A halo around the sun or moon is seen when the sun's light refracts through ice crystals in the high-level clouds. This often precedes a period of low pressure, which brings rain or snow with it.

- ✪ **'The higher the clouds, the better the weather.'** When the only clouds you can see are very high in the sky, this is a sign of dry air and high pressure, both of which signal dry weather.

- ✪ **'You can tell the temperature by counting a cricket's chirps.'** This sounds unlikely but it's true, and there's even a scientific formula for it, called Dolbear's Law. For any cowboys operating in Fahrenheit, you need to count the number of chirps in 15 seconds and then add 40. To find the temperature in Celsius, count the number of chirps in 8 seconds and add 5. So if a cricket chirps 20 times in 8 seconds, the temperature is 25 degrees Celsius.

TRAVELING IN A TEAM

If you're lacking in experience—and, heck, even if you have hundreds of trail miles under your cowboy belt—it's always safest to travel with friends, so that you can look out for each other and be there to support each other when things go wrong. Traveling alone can be satisfying, but in dangerous or unknown landscapes you'll never regret having a companion or two on the trail with you.

'ALWAYS CARRY A FLAGON OF WHISKEY IN CASE OF SNAKEBITE AND FURTHERMORE ALWAYS CARRY A SMALL SNAKE.'

W. C. FIELDS

ACTIVITY

TAKE A WALK ON THE WILDLIFE SIDE

When pressures are building up and you're feeling stressed, a great way to calm down and feel more like yourself again is to take a break from indoor life and give yourself a chance to experience the natural world. Being outside in nature helps us feel more grounded and connected to the wider environment of plants and animals, and the fresh breezes help to blow away those worries that can feel so big when we're stuck inside.

And the benefits of a walk don't have to be reserved for when you're feeling blue, of course. If you can, try to go on a little adventure every day, exploring a section of your neighborhood or making a circuit of your local park. Open your senses to the sights, sounds, and scents around you. You might see a gull nesting on a chimney stack, or a coyote strolling nonchalantly through a backyard. Over time, you'll see different flowers bloom in their seasons, and you'll see birds feeding their chicks and watching them fly off into adulthood. Placing your own life in this wider natural context can be a wonderful way to find a new perspective on your worries, and it can also help you to come up with new ideas. Give it a try today!

STOICISM AND MENTAL HEALTH

There's a lot to be said for stoicism, and it's certainly a noble aim to try to go through life with courage, moderation, a willingness to do the right thing, and the wisdom to choose the best way forward when things are looking complicated. However, being stoical does not mean that you have to bottle up all your problems and cope with them on your own.

When it comes to mental health, stoicism can be overrated, and it's often when we're at our lowest that we feel most unwilling to burden those around us with the sorrows that are weighing us down. But actually, a true stoic's courage comes to the fore at these times, by asking for help and allowing ourselves to be vulnerable in front of our friends and loved ones.

Just as you are always willing to help your friends and family when they need you, the chances are they will want to be there for you too in your moments of need, so don't be afraid to open up and seek help when you need it. And when your personal connections can't give you the support you require, there are professionals at the end of a phone or text message, or in a doctor's office, who are ready to listen and help. You don't need to suffer in silence: cowboys pull together, through the good times and the tough ones alike.

When we embrace the stoical values of cowboy life, we open ourselves up to bigger and bolder adventures—after all, the world is wider and the road stretches further ahead in front of us when we're brave enough to accept its invitation without saying 'no' and putting up barriers.

Sometimes the adventure lying ahead of us might not be an unmapped dusty trail through the hills; it could be a change of direction at work, a new hobby, or even a chance to make new friends by going somewhere you've never been before. Giving your inner stoic a chance to shine might make the scariness of these new challenges that little bit more manageable—it's certainly worth a try.

The natural world is full of wonders large and small, and taking yourself out on a mini adventure is a wonderful way to experience them and to practice your stoical skills along the way. Even a lunchtime exploration of a local park can reveal animals and plants you've never noticed before, and a weekend excursion to a nature reserve or countryside trail opens up even more possibilities. Fly your courageous flag and let your cowboy spirit lead you on a new path—who knows what you'll discover on your journey!

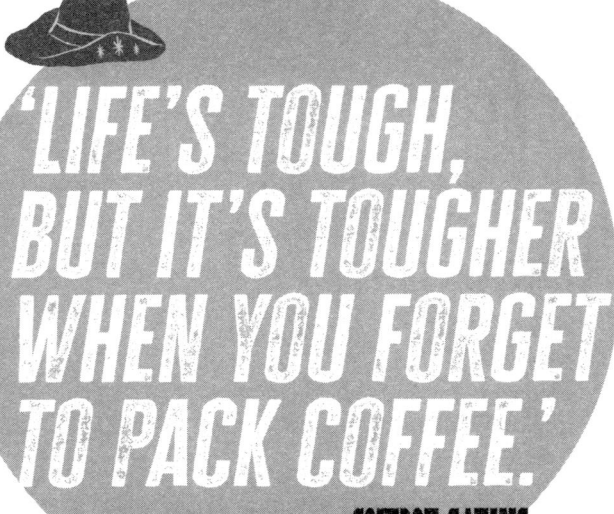

Home on the Range

HOME SWEET HOME

In 1862, the Homestead Act was passed by Congress, allowing any US citizen or any immigrant intending to become a citizen to set up a farm on 160 acres of unclaimed land. All they needed to do to claim the land for themselves was to pay a small filing fee. If they built a house, planted crops, and lived there continuously for five years, they would receive full title rights to the property. As a direct result of this legislation, over 80 million acres in the West were settled by new arrivals between 1862 and 1900.

The earliest ranches were built from whatever materials could be obtained locally, and they were not remotely grand. A single-storey log cabin would keep out the cold and did not take long to build, but you might have to live in your covered wagon or even in a tent while you were saving up for the timber and other materials. A finished home would keep out the elements, but it wouldn't be luxurious, as money for furnishings would be tight, and it's not as if there was a branch of IKEA nearby.

However, people still managed to add comfort to their ranch homes, despite all the challenges. By making the most delicious and satisfying meals they could and crafting objects to decorate the rooms, life became a little cozier and more enjoyable—and when you feel like that, even the most basic of dwellings can be a Home Sweet Home.

ADDING COWBOY FLAIR TO YOUR HOME

You may not live in a log cabin, but you can still add a touch of cowboy style to your home. Here are some ideas to bring a little of the West to every point of the compass.

The Navajo people of North America have been producing beautiful woven textiles for hundreds of years, and their blankets and rugs were highly prized by homemakers in the Old West. Some show depictions of people and animals, but most of them are typified by their striking geometric designs. A **Navajo blanket or rug** will bring warmth and style to your living room or bedroom.

If you visit some of your local second-hand shops, you may find some pre-loved **wooden chairs and tables** that will bring an old-fashioned sturdy charm to your home. If the wood has some scratches and dents after years of use, so much the better; with a little beeswax polish and some elbow grease their character will shine through and you will enjoy them for years to come.

A **cross-stitched sampler** is a perfect way to combine crafting with an inspirational message to share your values and make you and your guests feel at home. There are lots of kits and tutorials available to help you get your stitch on, but if you don't feel sampler-ready yet, you can find some lovely examples in antique shops and charity shops. Buying an older sampler is a really nice way to preserve and celebrate someone else's crafting skills, too.

THE WAY TO A COWBOY'S HEART

There were two things a hardworking cowboy longed for most during his or her long hours out in the ranch or on the trail: a good night's sleep and a satisfying meal. The former depended on the comfort offered by the ranch's bunkhouse—or when traveling, on the weather conditions for a night's cowboy camping. The latter was in the hands of perhaps the most important person on the ranch apart from the boss: the cook.

A ranch's cook held the mood of the cowboys in his hands. Though he kept himself apart from the rest of the workers, sleeping in his own cookshack rather than in the bunkhouse, he had the power to make the cowboys as happy as they could be—and a ranch with a good cook would be much more likely to keep the best cowhands from seeking pastures new.

Andy Adams (1859–1935) was a cowboy whose work took him along the cattle trails that led from Texas to Kansas and who later settled in Colorado. In his memoir *Cattle Trails* he recalled the importance of Little Jack Martin, his camp's cook:

If the way to rule men is through the stomach, Jack was a general who never knew defeat. The 'J+H' camp, where he presided over the kitchen, was noted for good living. Jack's domestic tastes followed him wherever he went, so that he surrounded himself at this camp with chickens, and a few cows for milk. During the spring months, when the boys were away on the various round-ups, he planted and raised a fine garden. Men returning from a hard month's work would brace themselves against fried chicken, eggs, milk, and fresh vegetables. After drinking alkali water for a month and living out of tin cans, who wouldn't love Jack? In addition to his garden, he always raised a fine patch of watermelons. This camp was an oasis in the desert. Every man was Jack's friend, and an enemy was an unknown personage. [...]

His best qualities shone their brightest when there were a dozen men around to cook for. When they ate heartily he felt he was useful. If a boy was sick, Jack could make a broth, or fix a cup of beef tea like a mother or sister. When he went out with the wagon during beef-shipping season, a pot of coffee simmered over the fire all night for the boys on night herd. Men going or returning on guard liked to eat. The bread and meat left over from the meals of the day were always left convenient for the boys. It was the many little things that he thought of which made him such a general favorite with every one.

COWBOY COOKING ON THE TRAIL

A trail drive could take cowboys away from their home ranch for months at a time, and it was vital that the whole team were able to eat properly along the way. The key to this, as well as a good cook, was the chuck wagon ('chuck' being slang for 'food'). This specially designed wagon contained all the cook's requirements, including a fold-out shelf at the back that could be used as a work surface, and several drawers containing everything the cowboys would need on the trail, including food supplies, cooking equipment, medicines, tools, and weapons.

The chuck wagon's legacy lives on in the modern cowboy era, thanks to the 'chuck box.' This is a box packed with food and cooking utensils that cowboys carry with them on their pickup trucks when they're out on a job. The chuck box is where you'll find everything you need to knock up a tasty lunch or dinner on the trail, and no journey is complete without one.

For a taste of the Old West as traveling cowboys might have experienced it, try one of these old-time recipes:

SON-OF-A-GUN STEW

Also known by a somewhat ruder name, this beef stew would be a nutritious treat for a hardworking cowboy, made from the meat and organs of one of the cattle traveling with them on the trail.

To make the stew, cut 2lb of beef, half a calf's heart and 1.5lb of calf liver into cubes and slice a calf's marrow gut into rings. Simmer these in a Dutch oven for 2–3 hours, seasoning with salt, pepper, and as much hot sauce as you prefer. Then cut the calf's sweetbreads and brain into small pieces, add them to the pot, and cook for 1 more hour.

COWBOY BEANS

To make this hearty dish, you'll need 2lb of pinto beans that have been soaked overnight, 2lb of salt pork or ham hock, 2 chopped onions, 4 tablespoons of sugar, green chilies, and tomato paste. The simplest cooking method is to simmer all the ingredients together for 3–4 hours until the beans are tender. Alternatively, you can fry the onions and chilies first, then move on to the simmering stage.

PEMMICAN

Pemmican is a mixture of rendered fat, dried and chopped meat, and dried fruit. It originates from the Indigenous people of North America, and its name is derived from a Cree word meaning 'fat' or 'grease.' This energy-rich food lasted well without needing refrigeration, and it was easy to transport. Its use as a survival food spread beyond North America to polar expeditions, army camps around the world, and aircraft emergency rations.

There are lots of variations of the recipe for pemmican, depending on the ingredients available or the tastes of the people eating it. For a classic version, combine 2lb of dried beef and ½lb of raisins and blend them to a fine paste in a food processor. Then pour in enough melted beef suet to hold the other ingredients together. Spread the mixture out on a baking sheet and let cool. When the pemmican has solidified, you can slice it into bars and store these until needed.

FROM 'A COW CAMP ON THE RANGE'

The cook is at the chuck-box
Whistling 'Heifers in the Green,'
Making baking powder biscuits, boys,
While the pot is biling beans.
The boys untie their bedding
And unroll it on the run,
For they are in a monstrous hurry
For the supper's almost done.

'Here's your bloody wolf bait,'
Cried the cook's familiar voice
As he climbed the wagon wheel
To watch the cowboys all rejoice.
Then all thoughts were turned from reverence
To a plate of beef and beans,
As we graze on beef and biscuits
Like yearlings on the range.

To the dickens with your city
Where they herd the brainless brats,
On a range so badly crowded
There ain't room to cuss the cat.
This life is not so sumptuous,
I'm not longing for a change,
For there is no place so homelike
As a cow camp on the range.

Anon.

SOMETHING TO WET THE WHISTLE

Cowboys liked to let their hair down when they reached the end of the trail and found a saloon with a generously stocked bar, but on the trail they generally had to live a pretty abstemious life. The cook may have carried some whiskey in his chuck wagon, but if so, this was purely for medicinal purposes—and some trail bosses didn't even allow this little luxury. In fact, in the late nineteenth century at the XIT Ranch in Texas, which covered three million acres, there was a very rigid policy: 'Employees are strictly forbidden the use of vinous, malt, spirituous, or intoxicating liquors, during their time of service with the Company.'

One non-alcoholic drink that helped to give cowboys an energy boost—just as it does for non-cowboys today—was a strong cup of coffee, brewed by the camp cook at the start of each day. When coffee first came to North America in the early seventeenth century, the beans were generally green, and it was hard to keep them fresh. Then, in the 1860s, the Arbuckle brothers patented a method of making long-life coffee beans, by roasting them and then coating each bean in a glaze of eggs and sugar. The Ariosa coffee brand made by the Arbuckles soon became a staple of the cowboy trail.

Trail cooks didn't have fancy coffee machines to brew up a beverage for their thirsty workers, but they made a great cup of coffee all the same. Here's how to make your very own cowboy coffee:

1. Grind coffee beans in a hand-cranked or electric grinder. You'll need 2 tablespoons of ground coffee for every 8fl oz/1 cup of water you use.

2. Boil your water. If you don't have a metal coffee pot and an open fire, you can boil water in a kettle and then pour it into a coffee pot.

3. Let the boiled water to cool for 30 seconds.

4. Add your ground coffee to the water and stir, then let the coffee rest for 2 minutes.

5. Stir again and let rest for another 2 minutes.

6. Once the coffee has brewed for 4 minutes, slowly pour a little cold water into the pot. This will help the coffee grounds to sink to the bottom of the pot.

7. Now gently pour the coffee into cups ready for drinking. If you pour slowly, the grounds will stay at the bottom of the pot and you'll have a delicious cup of cowboy coffee to enjoy.

A COWBOY'S GRACE

Eat the meat and leave the skin;
Turn up your plate and let's begin.
Yes, we'll come to the table
As long as we are able;
An' eat every damn thing
That seems sorta stable.

Anon.

'A COWBOY IS A PERSON WHO WOULD RATHER THROW A BULL THAN EAT BEANS WITH HIS KNIFE.'

CHARLES DORIAN

ACTIVITY

HOST A COWBOY-THEMED PARTY

Now that you've invited the spirit of cowboy living into your home, why not share the experience with friends and family by holding a cowboy-themed get-together? If you have an outdoor space, you can turn the event into a cookout, with ribs, sausages and corn cobs on the grill for everyone to enjoy—and you can make the preparations easier by asking guests to bring different foods with them, such as hot dog buns, salads, and sweet treats.

If you don't have any outdoor space, you can cook the meal indoors and still enjoy some campfire fun by toasting marshmallows over a candle (just make sure it's in a stable candleholder, for safety, and have a glass of water nearby in case you need to quench it quickly).

Ask everyone to attend in their finest cowboy outfits, with hats, bandanas, blue jeans, and cowboy boots, and you're sure to have the best rootin'-tootin' time together!

Back in the days of the Old West, cowboys and their families had to find their own ways to make the wildest places feel like home. With just the belongings they were able to carry by wagon and any furnishings they were able to craft themselves or buy from traveling traders, they managed to make a fresh start and create their own feeling of safety and coziness.

Perhaps it's worth taking on a little of this cowboy spirit in our own homes and appreciating the things we have instead of longing for newer versions. After all, it's not really the things we own that make us happy; it's the life we live, and the people we choose to spend it with.

Make your life a little more cowboy by celebrating the pleasures of home life, cooking up a hearty meal, and relaxing once the pots and pans have been cleaned and wrangled back into their proper places. And if you're going to cook up a hotpot, why not invite your friends round and enjoy it in their company? You don't have to have a full-on hoedown with your stew and beans—but on the other hand, it might be just the thing to blow away the cares of the day. Strike up the fiddle and let's get dancing!

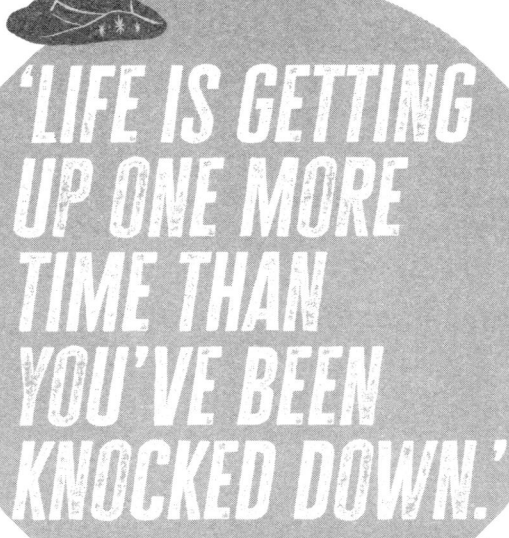

The Stage, the Page, & the Silver Screen

LARGER-THAN-LIFE COWBOY PERFORMERS

The cowboy has been an iconic figure ever since the heyday of the Old West and, in fact, the allure of a cowboy tale was felt just as strongly by actual cowboys as it was by people who lived thousands of miles away from cattle country, in villages, towns, and cities. Perhaps we all share a secret longing for the romance and adventure of the open prairie, where you have to rely on your horse and your own skills to reach the end of the trail—and if the action is a little more outrageous and dangerous than real cowboy life, no one's going to complain.

The first creators of the international cowboy myth started their careers on the ranches and battlefields and in the bars of the Wild West, before swapping their individual adventures for the public drama of the stage. These men and women would go on to create breathtaking daredevil performances, and many of them remain household names to this day.

William F. 'Buffalo Bill' Cody (1846–1917): Starting from the age of 11, William F. Cody's career encompassed cattle herding, fur trapping, gold mining, riding for the Pony Express, and scouting for the army. In 1872, he took part in a drama called *Scouts of the Prairie*, and discovered his calling as a showman. Then, in 1883, he put together his own show, *Buffalo Bill's Wild West*, a touring production featuring sharpshooters, horse-riding feats, and reenactments of stagecoach robberies and Indian attacks. The show traveled widely across North America and Europe, and was notable for featuring American Indian performers, including the Lakota chief, Sitting Bull.

Martha Jane Canary, 'Calamity Jane' (1852–1903): Martha Jane Canary lost both her parents in her teenage years and was left with the responsibility of looking after her five younger siblings. She took on a string of jobs, including dancehall girl, cook, nurse, ox team driver, and sex worker, and learned to be an expert sharpshooter. Her shooting skills earned her a place in *Buffalo Bill's Wild West* show in 1895. She was associated with 'Wild Bill' Hickok, though there are conflicting accounts of how close their relationship was, and they were united in death when Jane was buried next to him in Deadwood, South Dakota.

'I FIGURE IF A GIRL WANTS TO BE A LEGEND, SHE SHOULD JUST GO AHEAD AND BE ONE.'

CALAMITY JANE

'GOD INTENDED WOMEN TO BE OUTSIDE AS WELL AS MEN, AND THEY DO NOT KNOW WHAT THEY ARE MISSING WHEN THEY STAY COOPED UP IN THE HOUSE.'

ANNIE OAKLEY

Annie Oakley (1860–1926): Another famous performer of the Wild West was Annie Oakley, known as 'Little Sure Shot' in Buffalo Bill's shows and immortalized for twentieth-century audiences in the Irving Berlin musical *Annie Get Your Gun*. At the age of 15, Annie won a shooting competition by defeating the man she would later marry, Frank E. Butler. Her skills as a markswoman were truly exceptional: she could hit a coin tossed in the air and shoot a cigarette from her husband's mouth. While touring Europe with Buffalo Bill, she repeated this feat by shooting ash from the end of a cigarette held by Kaiser Wilhelm II.

Bill Pickett (1870–1932): Born in Texas, Bill Pickett was an African American cowboy with Cherokee ancestry who started working with longhorn cattle after leaving school in the fifth grade. As well as performing with Buffalo Bill, Pickett was also a famous rodeo star. His unique specialty was 'bulldogging,' which involved jumping from his horse, grabbing a steer by the neck or horns, then biting its lip and wrestling it to the ground.

COWBOYS IN THEATERLAND

Stories of cowboy life also found their place in the calmer world of the theater, with slightly less live ammunition and bareback horse riding than were found in the Wild West shows. In 1910, Giacomo Puccini's opera *La fanciulla del West*—or, in English, *The Girl of the Golden West*—opened at New York's Metropolitan Opera. Based on an earlier English-language play, it tells a tale of love, jealousy, and redemption set in California's Gold Rush, complete with a bandit, a sheriff, and a pure-hearted saloon owner, Minnie, who gives the work its title. Although not performed as often as his other operas, Puccini viewed this as his masterpiece, and many music critics share his opinion.

A play by Lynn Riggs premiered in 1931 that took its title from a folk song: *Green Grow the Lilacs*. The story, set in Indian Territory that would later become the state of Oklahoma, is a love triangle between a farm girl, a farmhand, and a cowboy, and features songs and dances alongside the spoken dialogue. *Green Grow the Lilacs* only ran for 64 performances, but it became an international smash hit when it was reborn in 1943 as the Rodgers and Hammerstein musical *Oklahoma!*. This optimistic and joyful show could not have been better timed to cheer up wartime audiences, and it played to packed theaters in New York and the wider US, as well as in London's West End, and several productions in Australia. To this day it is still a hugely popular work, with well-known songs including 'Oh, What a Beautiful Mornin',' 'The Surrey with the Fringe on Top,' and 'I Cain't Say No.'

READING THE RANGE

Cowboys have been galloping across the printed page for at least 150 years, delighting readers with tales of adventure and bravery. In the 1870s, Beadle's dime novels swept the US, entertaining readers with 'stories of Border Life and Character, Indian Warfare and Frontier Experience, Early Settlement Romance and Fact, Revolutionary Events and Incidents, Sea and Ship Life, &c., &c., &c.' in a cheap paperback binding. Who could resist tales such as *Little Thunderbolt; or, The Rangers of the Carolinas. A Tale of the Skinners and Cowboys* and *The Border Huntress; or, Wild Nat, the Gulch Terror*, all for just 10 cents? This series alone had 321 issues, and there were plenty of other publishers creating cheap, pocket-sized adventures for cowboys and city-dwellers alike.

A somewhat unlikely literary cowboy hero is the German author Karl May (1842–1912). May wrote more than 30 Western novels starring a cowboy called Old Shatterhand and his Apache friend Winnetou. These immediately caught the imagination of the German public for their celebration of the simple life in wild, natural surroundings and for the battles of their noble-hearted heroes against evil thugs and corrupt businessmen. Karl May is not widely known among English-speaking readers, but his books have sold over 200 million copies around the world and are still popular today.

POETS IN COWBOY HATS

Cowboy poetry is an art form whose history stretches back all the way to the days after the American Civil War, when cowboys first set out on their long cattle drives, heading west from Texas. Influenced by classic literature, oral storytelling, and the songs of the day, cowboy poetry is known for capturing with wit and honesty the authentic experiences of the men and women who traveled across the US with their herds.

In 1910, John Lomax published the collection *Cowboy Songs and Other Frontier Ballads*, with most of the included texts taken from anonymous sources, and which was praised by US President Theodore Roosevelt—a former 'dude' cowboy himself—as 'a work of real importance.' The poems in this collection include portraits of heroes and outlaws, descriptions of the rigors of a cowboy's working life, and ballads of shoot-outs, stampedes, and lost loves.

Cowboy poetry is still a very popular artform, and since 1985 it has been celebrated with an annual festival, the National Cowboy Poetry Gathering. This event is hosted by the Western Folklife Center in Elko, Nevada, and everyone is welcome: as the festival's official website says, 'It's not about what you wear or where you're from, it's about that cow town state of mind.'

ACTIVITY

WRITE YOUR OWN COWBOY POETRY

Are you feeling inspired by the cowboy poets? Then why not sit down with a notepad and write your own poem of cowboy life. If you haven't been lucky enough to trek across Montana on horseback or herd cattle in Kansas, don't worry—your poem can be based on an adventure, a journey, or even a mishap that has happened in your own life, and it will be just as exciting and gripping as that of any cowpoke. Remember, adventure is in the eye of the beholder—after all, if you can maintain your sanity after a commute involving pouring rain, a flat phone battery, and a rail-replacement bus, you are more than hero enough to match any cowboy traversing the rugged plains of the West.

Once your poetry fuse has been lit, the next step is to share your versifying verve with your friends or your book group! Poetry comes to life when it's performed, and though it may seem scary at first, your cowboy courage will see you through. If you're feeling uncertain, just think about how much you would like to hear your friends' poems—it stands to reason that they will enjoy yours just as much.

'THE RAMBLING COWBOY'

There was a rich old rancher who lived in the country by,
He had a lovely daughter on whom I cast my eye;
She was pretty, tall, and handsome, both neat and very fair,
There's no other girl in the country with her I could compare.

I asked her if she would be willing for me to cross the plains;
She said she would be truthful until I returned again;
She said she would be faithful until death did prove unkind,
So we kissed, shook hands, and parted, and I left my girl behind.

I left the State of Texas, for Arizona I was bound;
I landed in Tombstone City, I viewed the place all round.
Money and work were plentiful and the cowboys they were kind
But the only thought of my heart was the girl I left behind.

One day as I was riding across the public square
The mail-coach came in and I met the driver there;
He handed me a letter which gave me to understand
That the girl I left in Texas had married another man.

I turned myself all round and about not knowing what to do,
But I read on down some further and it proved the words were true.
Hard work I have laid over, it's gambling I have designed.
I'll ramble this wide world over for the girl I left behind.

Come all you reckless and rambling boys who have listened to this song,
If it hasn't done you any good, it hasn't done you any wrong;
But when you court a pretty girl, just marry her while you can,
For if you go across the plains she'll marry another man.

Anon.

THE GOOD, THE BAD, AND THE COWBOY: THE WILD WEST ON FILM

It is impossible to imagine the history of cinema without cowboys, and to even begin to sum up the impact of cowboys on the movies would take at least a whole book. We don't have quite that much space available, so instead, here are ten classic films that capture the best of the West on the big screen.

***Stagecoach* (1939):** Directed by John Ford and widely viewed as a masterpiece, this film made John Wayne into a major star. It tells the story of an eclectic group of nine strangers traveling by stagecoach from Arizona Territory to New Mexico in June 1880.

***My Darling Clementine* (1946):** Another John Ford movie, this time starring Henry Fonda as Wyatt Earp. Earp falls for his associate Doc Holliday's former girlfriend, the eponymous Clementine, in the events leading up to the shoot-out at the O.K. Corral.

***She Wore a Yellow Ribbon* (1949):** This is the middle film of John Ford's 'Cavalry Trilogy,' coming out between *Fort Apache* (1948) and *Rio Grande* (1950). John Wayne, playing older than his real age, portrays a veteran soldier on a final mission to stop a new conflict breaking out between Native Americans and the army, in the aftermath of Custer's Last Stand.

***High Noon* (1952):** Starring Gary Cooper and Grace Kelly and directed by Fred Zinnemann, this film won four Oscars for its real-time depiction of a man having to choose between leaving with his new bride or facing off with a vengeance-seeking criminal, while the rest of the town hides behind its own cowardice.

***Shane* (1953):** Based on a 1949 novel by Jack Schaefer, *Shane* stars Alan Ladd as a gunslinger with a mysterious past who is hired by homesteaders in Wyoming Territory to protect their isolated farm from the land baron who wants to evict them illegally by force.

The Good, the Bad, and the Ugly* (1966):** Perhaps the most famous cowboy film of all time, this is the third movie in Sergio Leone's ***Dollars Trilogy, after *A Fistful of Dollars* (1964) and *For a Few Dollars More* (1965). Clint Eastwood is unmatched as the anti-hero bounty-hunter who forms an

uneasy alliance with Mexican bandit Tuco, played by Eli Wallach, and Lee Van Cleef's mercenary 'Angel Eyes.'

***Butch Cassidy and the Sundance Kid* (1969):** Based loosely on the true story of Robert LeRoy Parker and Harry Longabaugh, and starring Paul Newman as Parker ('Butch') and Robert Redford as Longabaugh ('Sundance'), this action-packed adventure tells the story of two outlaw friends who attempt to go straight, with limited success.

'STORYTELLING WAS A WAY TO SEE THE WORLD BIGGER THAN THE ONE YOU WERE LOOKING AT, AND THAT HAD GREAT APPEAL FOR ME.'

ROBERT REDFORD

***Blazing Saddles* (1974):** This spoof to end all spoofs was directed by Mel Brooks, and its humor ranges from the infantile, such as its symphony of bean-induced cowboy farting, to the pointedly satirical, in its portrayal of the prejudice meted out to the new Black sheriff of the town of Rock Ridge, played by Cleavon Little.

***Unforgiven* (1992):** Winning Oscars for Best Picture and Best Director, *Unforgiven* stars an older Clint Eastwood as an outlaw-turned-farmer who takes on a bounty-hunting job to avenge a sex worker who was attacked by two cowboys.

***No Country for Old Men* (2007):** This film by brothers Joel and Ethan Coen is based on Cormac McCarthy's 2005 novel of the same title. It stars Tommy Lee Jones as a sheriff in pursuit of Javier Bardem's hitman Anton Chigurh. Chigurh himself is on the trail of a Vietnam War veteran played by Josh Brolin, who has discovered a haul of drug money and made the life-changing decision to keep it.

Heroes and villains of the Wild West have been celebrated in every known art form, in a long line going back to the days of the first cowboys and ranchers. It is perhaps the very real sense of having to rely on your own physical and mental strength, and your connection with the natural world, that remains so appealing.

In the mid-nineteenth century, as cowboys were making their way west through every kind of challenge and obstacle, thousands of other people in towns and cities were learning to adapt to an increasingly industrialized way of life. The march of technology has brought us comfort in many ways, but when our daily adventures involve nothing more adrenaline-provoking than lassoing emails and wrangling customers, it's no wonder that the stories of true cowboys keep rounding us up again.

We can still escape to the world of cowboys, sheriffs, and bandits, thanks to the books, films, and shows that celebrate them. Their tales of resilience, bravery, and sheer refusal to fit in with society's expectations can inspire us to be more cowboy every day, standing up for what's right, even when the odds seem stacked against us.

A Cowboy Chorus

THE ORIGINAL COWBOY BALLADS

Cowboys and music have belonged together from the beginnings of the Western cattle trails right up to the present day. On the long journeys out of Texas, anyone who could carry a tune or play an instrument was welcome, and not just because of the entertainment value for the rest of the team. Music was an important tool for keeping the cattle happy: at night, cowboys would sing lullabies so the cattle would remain calm amid the unknown dangers in the dark; then, during the day, a jaunty song would help keep them moving at a decent pace.

Often based on folk melodies, songs were written to capture the unique excitements and dangers of the cowboy way of life, and as people sang them in the towns and railheads of the West, they spread widely, picking up new verses—some of them bawdier than others—with each

new community they reached. Two anthologies published at the start of the twentieth century, *Songs of the Cowboys*, edited by Nathan Howard Thorp, and *Cowboy Songs and Other Frontier Ballads*, collected by John Lomax, ensured that future generations could appreciate the music and poetry of the cowboys.

This song, first published in 1912, tells the story of a man who is as skilled with his gun as he is with a song to lull his animals to sleep:

'RAGTIME COUNTRY JOE'

Out in Arizona
Where the bad men are,
And the only friend to guide you

Is an evening star,
The roughest and the toughest
Man by far
Is Ragtime Cowboy Joe.
He got his name from singing
To the cows and sheep
Every night they say
He sings the herd to sleep
In a basso
Rich and deep,
Crooning soft and low.

He always sings
Raggy music to the cattle
As he swings
Back and forward in the saddle
On a horse
That is syncopated gaited
And there's such a funny meter
To the roar of his repeater.
How they run
When they hear that fellow's gun
Because the Western folks all know
He's a high-faluting, scooting, shooting,
Son of a gun from Arizona,
Ragtime Cowboy Joe.

Grant Clarke, Lewis F. Muir, and Maurice Abrahams

THE CLEAN-CUT SINGING COWBOY

Starting in the 1920s, a new type of cowboy found his place on the movie screen and on the nation's gramophone: the singing cowboy. With a clean-shaven face and an equally clean white hat, this wholesome, heroic figure traveled with a guitar on his back and was always ready to break into song.

Gene Autry (see page 38) is one of the most famous of the singing cowboys, thanks to his more than 90 film appearances and his long-running television show (in which he helped to promote the cowboy code, as we saw in Chapter 2). As well as being known for cowboy-themed songs such as 'Back in the Saddle Again' and 'Mule Train,' Gene Autry was also the first to perform the Christmas classics 'Rudolph the Red-Nosed Reindeer' and 'Frosty the Snowman.'

Another archetypal singing cowboy was Roy Rogers (1911–1998), who earned the nickname 'King of the Cowboys.' Under his original name, Leonard Slye, he appeared in *Tumbling Tumbleweeds*, a 1935 movie starring Gene Autry, and he soon became Autry's key competitor for the crooning cowboy crown. Like Autry, Rogers made dozens of movies during his career and also hosted a television show bearing his name. Some of his most popular songs are 'Don't Fence Me In,' 'Happy Trails,' and 'Tumbling Tumbleweeds.'

'DON'T EVER UNDERESTIMATE THE POWER OF A GOOD SONG, A GOOD HORSE AND A GOOD HAT.'

GENE AUTRY

A COUNTRY AND WESTERN HALL OF FAME

So far we've focused on songs by or about cowboys, which generally come under the heading of 'Western music.' But this is just one subgenre within the wider universe of 'Country and Western music,' and I couldn't let this chapter pass without visiting some of the biggest stars of the country scene. These singers have created evergreen torch songs, ballads, and upbeat songs that get the whole room dancing—and when you walk past a karaoke bar you will often hear one of their timeless classics being recreated, with heartfelt enthusiasm if not pinpoint accuracy. What is it that we love so much about this music: is it the melodies, the emotions, or the iconic performances with cowboy boots, guitars, and sequins? The alchemy behind a great country song keeps drawing us in, time and time again.

Hank Williams (1923–1953): Born in Alabama as Hiram Williams, and known as the 'Hillbilly Shakespeare,' Hank Williams left a lasting legacy on the country scene, even though his recording career lasted only six years. Famed for the emotion he brought to songs such as 'I'm So Lonesome I Could Cry,' 'Your Cheatin' Heart,' and 'Lovesick Blues,' he died tragically young but continues to inspire performers today.

Patsy Cline (1932–1963): Like Hank Williams, Patsy Cline left the stage far too soon, when she died in a plane crash at the age of just 30. Her career combined country songs with a pop-like performance style, and she was the first solo female performer to be inducted into the Country Music Hall of Fame, in 1973. Some of her timeless hits are 'Walkin' After Midnight' (my personal karaoke favorite), 'Crazy,' and 'I Fall to Pieces.'

Johnny Cash (1932–2003): Famed as 'The Man in Black,' Johnny Cash forged his own unique career through songs such as 'I Walk the Line' and 'Ring of Fire,' sung in a deep bass-baritone voice. He used his high profile to advocate for prison reform and for the rights of Native Americans, and his albums *Johnny Cash at Folsom Prison* and *Johnny Cash at San Quentin*, recorded live during performances for prison inmates, both reached No. 1 on the *Billboard* country album chart in the US. He would later form a supergroup called The Highwaymen with fellow music legends Kris Kristofferson, Waylon Jennings, and Willie Nelson.

Willie Nelson (1933–): A star of outlaw country music, Willie Nelson's hits include 'On the Road Again,' 'Always on My Mind,' and 'Blue Eyes Crying in the Rain'—and on top of this, he also wrote 'Crazy' for Patsy Cline. His decades-long career has seen him collaborate with performers from across the musical spectrum, from Julio Iglesias to Snoop Dogg, and he continues to delight packed concert venues in his 90s. Nelson recently revealed

that he has a black belt in GongKwon Yusul, a Korean martial art, proving that he is a force to be reckoned with both on and off the stage.

Dolly Parton (1946–): How do you even begin to sum up the achievements of Dolly Parton? With over 100 million record sales, 11 Grammys, 25 No. 1 singles on the *Billboard* country music chart, beloved starring roles in films such as *9 to 5*, a successful theme park, and on top of all this, a literacy programme that sends a free book to 850,000 children every month, Dolly Parton is a phenomenon—and one who has all too often been underestimated thanks to her bubbly blonde persona. With hits like 'Jolene,' 'I Will Always Love You,' '9 to 5,' and 'Coat of Many Colors,' among her thousands of songs, she has created a truly unique musical legacy.

KEEPIN' IT COWBOY IN THE TWENTY-FIRST CENTURY

While country and western music will always have its own devoted audience, the cowboy sound has also been a strong influence on many mainstream pop performers, particularly in the 2020s. Here are just a few of the singers who regularly walk on the cowboy side of life.

⭐ Having started her career in Nashville as a country singer with her self-titled debut album, Taylor Swift has progressed through many different musical styles throughout her career, but she hasn't abandoned the cowboy dream. Her ninth studio album, *evermore*, released in 2020, featured a song called 'cowboy like me,' a mellow ballad in which two con artists fall in love in a story that ends in heartbreak.

⭐ Beyoncé's 2024 album *Cowboy Carter* is rooted in country music while still being at heart a pure Beyoncé creation. The album blends elements of country pop, Americana, and outlaw country, and features performances from Black country performers including Shaboozey, Tanner Adell, and Willie Jones. 'Texas Hold 'Em,' one of the album's hit singles, celebrates the role of Black musicians in country music, and Beyoncé's cover version of 'Jolene' creates a direct connection between two of America's biggest musical icons.

⭐ The Irish artist CMAT, also known as Ciara Mary-Alice Thompson, has been inspired by cowboy music and imagery throughout her musical career, and often performs in colorful cowboy boots. Songs such as 'I Wanna Be a Cowboy, Baby' and 'Nashville' refer directly to the world of country music, while the video for 'Every Bottle (Is My Boyfriend)' is set in a saloon straight out of a Spaghetti Western.

⭐ Since shooting to international fame in recent years, Chappell Roan has wowed concertgoers and video viewers alike with her highly experimental haute couture costumes, but perhaps her most iconic fashion accessory is the cowboy hat, as featured in the video for her 2020 single 'Pink Pony Club' and the epic cowboy clown rodeo performance of the same song at the 2025 Grammys. Her 2025 single 'The Giver' continued the country and western mood with its toe-tapping fiddle melodies and represented Roan's decision to create 'a song of joy' about lesbian love from the music genre that had accompanied her closeted upbringing in Missouri. I think we can all agree she got the job done.

ACTIVITY

COWBOY KARAOKE

The world of country and western music is vast, with a song for every mood and situation you might find yourself in, and you can make the most of this rich variety of songs with your very own cowboy karaoke session.

Fire up your favorite music streaming service or dive into YouTube, search for singalong versions of the classic country songs, and then sing your heart out, either with a karaoke microphone or simply making the most of the acoustics of your living room or kitchen—anywhere can be a karaoke booth when you're in the mood to sing! If you can't find a bespoke karaoke version of the song you want, just turn on the lyric captions and sing along with Dolly, Johnny, or whoever else is your inspiration today.

Karaoke is always fun with friends, but there's a lot to be said for a cathartic sing-your-heart-out solo session, too, as my car interior knows all too well. Why not try both options? And experts say that you will enjoy your singing even more if you are wearing a cowboy hat, cowboy boots, a fringed jacket, and other garments decorated with sequins. (Okay, it's me, I'm the 'experts' in this scenario—but it's 100 per cent true!)

Here's a menu of songs to get you started, tailored to the vibe you're feeling in your karaoke session.

I'm in the mood to party: 'If You've Got the Money I've Got the Time' by Lefty Frizzell

I'm an incurable romantic: 'Love Story' by Taylor Swift

I want to run away with a cowboy: 'Cowboy Take Me Away' by the Dixie Chicks (now The Chicks)

I'm devoted to you: 'I Walk the Line' by Johnny Cash

We belong together (duet): 'Islands in the Stream' by Dolly Parton and Kenny Rogers

I love my horse: 'A Four Legged Friend' by Roy Rogers

I love traveling alone: 'Wand'rin' Star' by Lee Marvin

I love traveling with my friends: 'On the Road Again' by Willie Nelson

I haven't got much but I'm happy all the same: 'King of the Road' by Roger Miller

I'm heartbroken: 'Crazy' by Patsy Cline

I'm lonely: 'I'm So Lonesome I Could Cry' by Hank Williams

I'm feeling melancholy: 'Wichita Lineman' by Glen Campbell

I'm in the wrong job: 'Should've Been a Cowboy' by Toby Keith

I miss the old days: 'The Last Cowboy Song' by The Highwaymen

I love telling an epic story: 'The Devil Went Down to Georgia' by Charlie Daniels

I want to be a famous singer: 'Rhinestone Cowboy' by Glen Campbell

If you don't like my singing, you are wrong: 'Mean' by Taylor Swift

I want to sing the best country song of all time: 'Jolene' by Dolly Parton

The music of the cowboys has stood the test of time, coming down to us from the heartfelt lullabies and campfire songs of the original men and women who traversed the Wild West in the nineteenth century all the way to Beyoncé's *Cowboy Carter Tour* of 2025, and its appeal seems certain to endure.

Cowboy songs and country music speak to us all in different ways. Some of us are drawn to songs of adventure and the open road, while others find solace in ballads of heartbreak and loneliness. Perhaps there's something in the honest authenticity of a singer with an acoustic guitar that cuts through our emotional defences, reaching directly into our hearts, or maybe it's the soaring, lilting voices of country music's most famous stars that help us to see our troubles as ripples in a vast ocean of shared experiences, elevated and eased through the power of music.

Whatever your musical taste, there's a country song out there that will speak to you, lulling you when you're sad, spurring you on when you need encouragement, and dancing with you when you're feeling joyful. With the right tune playing, you can be more cowboy every day—and if you join in with the song, life will feel even better.

'A GOOD OLD RODEO NEVER HURT ANYONE.'

TAYLOR KITSCH

When the Work's All Done

AT THE END OF THE DAY

Cowboys have to work hard for a living, caring for their horses, keeping their cattle safe, and doing the 101 jobs that keep a ranch going from day to day, but when the day's work is done, it's time to kick back and relax—at least until the work begins again tomorrow.

Out on the trail, opportunities for fun would be limited to whatever the cowboys could come up with, such as singing trail songs, telling tall stories, swapping jokes, and enjoying some music if anyone had a guitar, fiddle, or harmonica with them. They also had unrivaled star-filled skies to contemplate, with no city lights to obscure the view. Still, every cowboy looked forward to the end of the trail, when they would finally enter a real town and have the chance to mix with new people, have a drink or two, and kick their heels up for a little while.

TO THE SALOON!

Even if they were planning wild times ahead, the average cowboy would probably have another priority in mind when they rode into town after weeks on horseback: a bath and a shave. Cleanliness was not easily achieved on the trail, with limited access to water and long, dusty days of hard work keeping cowboys busy, and nobody would want to enter a saloon covered in weeks'-worth of grime. As well as hot water and soap, many cowboys would be looking for a new set of clothes, as the ones they'd been wearing every day for the whole journey would no doubt be entirely worn out.

Having found a tub in a rooming-house and a new outfit in a local store, a cowboy could then start enjoying all the other delights that a town had to offer. These might include street musicians, hawkers, and impromptu cattle auctions, and for the more devout visitor there would also be religious services to attend.

But for many new arrivals the primary destination would be the nearest saloon, where a wide variety of alcoholic beverages would be available, not to mention opportunities for gambling and making arrangements with sex workers.

Businesses were quick to make the most of the money in a cowboy's pocket, and in Dodge City, Kansas, saloons and stores stayed open for 24 hours a day to ensure that every dollar possible ended up in their cash registers.

One myth about the saloons of the Old West is that they had the kind of slatted, half-length swinging doors that we see in classic movies; in fact, photographs of real saloons from the cowboy era show perfectly normal, solid doors that go all the way from the floor to the ceiling. Another myth is the idea that gunfights were regular occurrences in the saloons cowboys frequented; in reality, many towns had local laws saying that cowboys had to check their weapons in at the local sheriff's office or at their hotel, and it was rare for people to carry guns into a saloon.

ACTIVITY

HOST YOUR VERY OWN OLD WEST SALOON NIGHT

If you're ready for a night of old-time fun the way cowboys used to do it, why not invite your friends round to your own DIY saloon? Here's what you'll need:

GUESTS

A barkeep: Okay, so in an ideal world you'll take turns serving the drinks, but this is a great opportunity for one of you to bring out your best black bow tie and waistcoat combo over a white shirt, and if you can wax your hair down with a smart center-parting and apply an elegant moustache (or style your own, if you already have one), then you'll really look the part. Make sure you keep an eye on new arrivals, to see who's likely to cause trouble.

A sheriff or marshal: Because *someone* is always going to cause trouble, and that barkeep can't keep order without a law man or woman on their side.

A diverse cast of cowboys, gamblers, swindlers, traveling preachers, and people of ill repute: Your friends will know who they are, and will dress accordingly.

SURROUNDINGS

A bar: This can be the kitchen counter, a dining table, or anything you can stand bottles and glasses on.

A gambling table: A coffee table is ideal for this—you just need enough space for cards and poker chips. As well as playing party classics like blackjack and poker (for matches, not for money!), take time before the event begins to look up the rules of Faro, the game that once ruled the cowboy saloon. It is wordy to explain but simple to play, and it has the benefit of giving the players relatively decent odds of winning.

Drinking music: Ideally, you'll have someone rattling out a cheerful polka on a slightly out-of-tune piano, but if the pianist doesn't show, you can crank out a playlist of ragtime melodies on your wind-up Bluetooth speaker instead and the effect will be just as pleasing.

Once you are all set up and your motley bunch of cowboys and their associates has arrived, settle down for an evening of real old-time cowboy entertainment! Watch out for brawls and showdowns, and be sure to call in the sheriff if there's any funny business. Finally, make sure everyone gets on the right horse at the end of the night before they ride back into the twenty-first century again.

The dust riz fast and furious; we all jes galloped round,
Till the scenery got so giddy that T Bar Dick was downed.
We buckled to our partners and told 'em to hold on,
Then shook our hoofs like lightning until the early dawn.
Don't tell me 'bout cotillions, or germans. No sir-ee!
That whirl at Anson City jes takes the cake with me.
I'm sick of lazy shufflin's, of them I've had my fill,
Give me a frontier break-down backed up by Windy Bill.
McAllister ain't nowhere, when Windy leads the show;
I've seen 'em both in harness and so I ought ter know.
Oh, Bill, I shan't forget yer, and I oftentimes recall
That lively gaited sworray – the Cowboy's Christmas Ball.

'The Cowboy's Christmas Ball,' Anon.

'RODEO AIN'T NO ORDINARY LIFE BUT A COWBOY AIN'T NO ORDINARY MAN.'

TRACY BYRD

LET'S GO TO THE RODEO!

The highlight events of the cowboy year in the early days of the cattle trade were the roundups of spring and fall, when cowboys would ride out to locate scattered stock and gather them in. This task required tenacity, speed, and skill, as cowboys had to identify cows with the correct brand mark, rope and brand young calves, and cooperate with cowboys from other ranches in sorting out whose animals were whose.

This activity was known by Spanish speakers by a word meaning a 'surrounding,' and it's a word now used widely in English too: *rodeo*. Cowboys liked to show off their roping and riding maneuvers, and the event soon evolved into a social gathering where they could perform in front of an audience. The first rodeos were informal events, but by the late nineteenth century rodeos had become professional public entertainments, and rodeo skills were also featured in the traveling Wild West shows run by Buffalo Bill and his competitors.

Today, rodeos continue to attract fearless performers and huge crowds, not just in North America but also in Australia, Brazil, Mexico, Guyana, the Philippines, and beyond, and rodeo has even been named the official state sport of the US states of South Dakota, Texas, and Wyoming. The two biggest rodeos in North America are the National Finals Rodeo, held annually in Paradise,

Nevada, in the first week of December, and the Calgary Stampede, which takes place every July in Alberta, Canada.

CLASSIC RODEO EVENTS

Here are the seven key events featured at the National Finals Rodeo, known by many as the 'Super Bowl of Rodeo.' Other rodeos have similar programmes, with variations and additions depending on local traditions. Although women have a long history of participation and skill as rodeo performers, many events today are only open to male competitors, with the exception of barrel racing, which is a women-only sport, and some of the roping events.

Bareback riding: In this event, a rider must stay on the back of a bucking horse for 8 seconds, with only a leather rigging made from two straps that go round the horse's body to hold on to. They receive a score out of 100, with half the points coming from the rider's skill and the other half based on how wildly the horse bucks.

Steer wrestling: In a feat that remains unbelievable even when you see it with your own eyes, this event involves a rider jumping off a galloping horse, grabbing a steer, and wrestling it to the ground—ideally in under 4 seconds.

Team roping: In a callback to the cowboy practice of roping a cow ready to be branded, this team event has two riders—known as a header and a heeler—both carrying lassos. The

header throws his rope around a steer's horns, and the heeler uses his rope to catch the steer's hind legs. Working together, the two ropers pull the steer to the ground as quickly as possible—the world record is 3.2 seconds.

Saddle bronc riding: This event is similar to bareback riding, except that the horse wears a saddle. The rider holds onto the horse's reins with one hand, and the other hand must stay in the air. As with the bareback event, the rider must stay on the bucking horse for 8 seconds, and the score is based equally on the rider's skill and the horse's wildness.

Tie-down roping: In this solo event, a rider lassos a calf around the neck, then dismounts and throws the animal to the ground. Finally, he ropes three of the calf's legs and throws his arms up in the air to stop the clock.

Barrel racing: This women-only event is a test of speed and skill, in which a rider races her horse as fast as possible around a course marked out by barrels. Horse and rider must skilfully loop around the barrels, without knocking any of them over.

Bull riding: The breathtaking finale of every rodeo is the bull riding event. Just like the bareback and saddle bronc events, a rider has to stay seated on a bucking bull for 8 seconds, holding on with only one hand, and receiving points based on his own skills and the wildness of the bull.

It takes huge dedication to be a professional rodeo performer, as the investment required for equipment, travel, and healthcare is substantial and the chance of winning enough to earn a living is slim. On top of all this, there is the significant risk of being seriously injured while practicing or performing in these highly risky events. But despite these very real challenges, rodeo performers are more than willing to tackle the financial and physical costs of their sport in order to put on a show to remember.

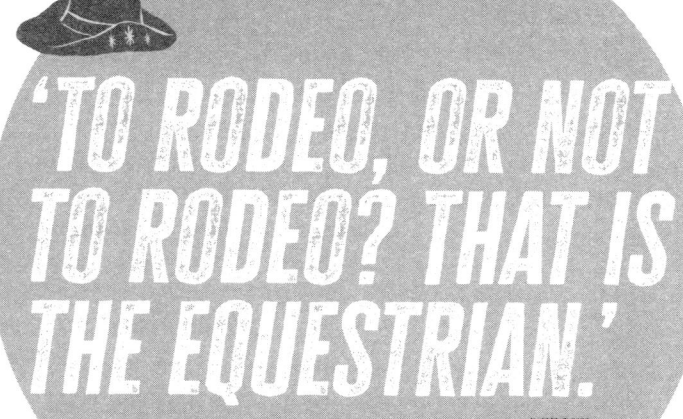

BE MORE Cowboy

Cowboys of old faced innumerable dangers, from bandits and poisonous snakes to accidents on the trail and diseases with few effective treatments, and their working hours were long and hard. But despite all this, they found time to enjoy themselves when the working day was done—perhaps it's one of the most universal human characteristics, the need to take a break and smile every now and then.

Each of us has our own preference when it comes to resting and recharging: some people are energized by hitting the bars and painting the town red; some are drawn to arts and crafts, or storytelling round the fire; while others find the deepest comfort in stargazing in silence, alone in the beauty of the natural world.

Whatever kind of work fills your days, it's vital to give yourself time to recover from the stresses the world gives you and to step away from your daily worries for a little while. Letting down your hair and spending time together in laughter with people you love is what gives you the fuel you need to be more cowboy. Then you can climb back in the saddle with a spring in your step tomorrow, ready for whatever the day has in store.

It's been a wild ride through the cowboy world, with all its highlights, high jinks, and history, but we've reached the end of the trail and it's time for me to bid you a fond farewell and ride off into the sunset. I hope you've enjoyed exploring the prairies with me, experiencing the best of cowboy life for twenty-first-century travelers.

Whether you spend your days on horseback or on two feet, I hope this little trek across the Wild West has inspired you to embrace the very best of the cowboy way of life: freedom, independence, boldness, integrity, and a willingness to see the good in everyone you meet along the trail.

So long, friend, and keep smiling till we meet again! May every day give you a chance to Be More Cowboy.

Under the star-studded Canopy vast,
Camp-fire and coffee and comfort at last,
Bacon that sizzles and crisps in the pan,
After the round-up smells good to a man.
Stories of ranchers and rustlers retold,
Over the Pipe as the embers grow cold,
Those are the times that old memories play,
Make me a Cowboy again for a day.

from 'Make Me a Cowboy Again for a Day,' Anon.